Muzoon

Muzoon

A SYRIAN REFUGEE SPEAKS OUT

MUZOON ALMELLEHAN

with WENDY PEARLMAN

ALFRED A. KNOPF
NEW YORK

I dedicate this book to my parents,
siblings, friends, and everyone who has believed
in my voice and helped me in my journey.

I also dedicate this book to people who believe in themselves
and do not give up on their dreams. Those whose
determination is greater than their fears. And those who
are trying to sow goodness in a world full of tragedies.

Contents

Muzoon

Prologue

This is my story. But it's also a window into many other stories.

It's also the story of my country, Syria.

When I was young, the people of Syria started speaking up and demanding more freedoms. But those peaceful demonstrations evolved into a conflict that has killed over six hundred thousand people. The war forced more than half of Syria's population, about twelve million people, to flee their homes. I am just one of them.

This is also the story of being a refugee.

Today, eighty-three million people around the world are displaced from their homes. Each has a unique story of loss and hope. My own journey has taught me that a refugee is not a type of person. It is someone in a kind of situation that could happen to anyone. One day you're a kid playing sports and watching cartoons. The next day there is war and you have to leave for a refugee camp. I didn't choose these things, but they happened to me and they have been my greatest teachers. They taught me to appreciate every opportunity and take nothing for granted. If you are not a refugee, I hope that my story gives you some sense of what it is like. If you are a refugee, I hope that my story reminds you to take pride in yourself and your journey.

This is also the story of being a kid.

Growing up is filled with challenges. Many things seem unfair or just don't make sense. There are so many things that we wish we could change but we can't. It is natural to feel frustrated or angry. But facing difficulties makes us realize all the strength we have inside. Today, whenever I feel doubt, I remember my younger self and the problems that she managed to overcome. It was the hard times, much more than the good ones, that gave me drive and determination.

There were times when I felt like the only things I had were my voice and my refusal to give up. I discovered that I could do a lot with those things.

I wrote this book because I believe that you can do a lot, too.

Thank you for reading my story.

PART I

HOME

October 2010

I like to remember my home in the time before the war began. When my cousins and I ran in and out of each other's houses and played soccer in the street. When our family gathered on the rooftop on warm evenings or came together to harvest the olives from the trees in our grove. I remember my grandmother's cooking, and the time my aunt and I made the worst harissa *cake ever. . . .*

Chapter 1

"Motorcycle!" my brother yelled.

I came to a full stop. I had brought the ball the distance of three houses. The rocks that we used as goal markers were nearly within reach. But when you played soccer in the street, you had to be ready to pause for traffic.

I placed my foot on the ball and looked right and left. No motorcycles.

"Tricked you!" Mohammed crowed, stealing the ball. He turned toward the rocks at the other end of the street.

I ran after him as fast as I could. My cousins Tayyim and Razi picked up speed behind me. Tayyim rushed to defend our goal. Razi positioned himself in case Mohammed decided to pass. I caught up within a breath of Mohammed, but he dodged my kick. I ran harder and reached my foot out long. This time, I heard the plastic of my flip-flop thump the ball. I pushed him out of the way.

The ball was now back under my control, and I wasn't about to lose it again. I went flying toward the rocks of our goal. Al-l-l-lmost there—kick! The ball sailed between the two rocks.

"Goal!" I shouted, pumping both fists overhead.

"Ughhhh," Mohammed groaned, his head dropping into his hands.

I was twelve and my brother Mohammed was exactly one year and eleven days younger than me. We were so close, you'd have thought we were twins. At the same time, we were always jealous of each other. If I got ketchup-flavored potato chips, he demanded ketchup-flavored potato chips. If he drank tea, I wanted to drink tea. And I don't even like tea! My three cousins closest in age were also boys, which made me the only girl in our pack of five.

Soccer was our obsession. We didn't really know the rules, so we made up our own. Still, we took the game very seriously. Whoever lost could expect to be taunted.

Mohammed was usually on a team with Razi, who was only a few months younger than me. I paired up with our other cousin Tayyim. Tayyim's older brother Mansour sometimes joined us, too. Mansour was the largest and strongest among us. He kicked the ball so hard that it scared me—not that I would admit it. So it was fine with me if he was absent. That meant I was the oldest and the one in charge, which was how I liked it.

Mohammed and I got into plenty of arguments. But if either of us got into an argument with one of our cousins, we became a united front. We wouldn't allow our cousins to come to our house. We'd declare our own fields and groves off limits. They would do the same to us. If one of them set foot on our property, we would demand an explanation. Or we would get back at them by entering their fields, even if we had to sneak there in the middle of the night.

One epic fight began after Mohammed and I planted a watermelon seed. Mohammed had a knack with plants, and he carefully tended this one until there was a big watermelon, almost ripe. Mansour talked about how tasty it would be, and how he couldn't wait to get a slice. When we woke up one morning and found it missing, we immediately knew the thief. Mohammed and I marched across the field to his house, and I gave him our signal to show that we were refusing to speak to him: I put my index finger to my tongue and thrust it toward the ground. Usually our angry silences lasted only hours. But the War of the Watermelon lasted weeks.

Even our parents respected our feuds. If we were in a fight with Tayyim and Mansour, Uncle Adnan and Aunt Ayida wouldn't bring them when they came to visit. Dad wouldn't take us if he went to visit them.

Then we would reconcile, and there was nothing our parents could do to keep us apart.

I grabbed the ball, and the four of us sat on the side of the road.

"Fake motorcycle is a new one," I said, kicking dirt in Mohammed's direction. He was always inventing new ways to cheat.

He grinned and batted his eyelashes. In our baby portraits we all had long eyelashes. While everyone else's eyes caught up with their lashes, Mohammed's remained outsized.

"Yeah, you usually just claim a broken flip-flop," Tayyim added.

Someone's flip-flop fell apart at least once a week, so calling out a ripped shoe was a believable way to halt the game when you were about to lose.

I brushed the dirt off my T-shirt, which was bright green with a large number 10 on the back. "I don't want to play with cheaters." I stood up, taking the ball with me.

"Come on, Muzoon. Let's keep going," Razi begged.

"No, I'm going home." I started walking away, ignoring the pleas behind me. When I got a foot from the stone markers, I put the ball down and shot it straight between them.

"Goal!" I shouted as I jumped up and down. One of my flip-flops slipped off and sailed through the air.

"That's not fair!" Mohammed wailed.

Okay, yes. I cheated sometimes, too.

Chapter 2

It was around two p.m.—time for all of us to go to our re-
spective houses for lunch. Razi lived a few minutes in one
direction and Tayyim a few minutes in the other. My family
lived in the middle, in a house that Dad built after we were
born. When Mohammed and I got to our door, the aroma of
mint, garlic, and cilantro greeted us. *"Shish barak,"* we said at
the same time.

Our grandmother had prepared the traditional stew of
meat dumplings boiled in yogurt. Jadati (my grandmother)
and Jidi (my grandfather) had grown up as Bedouins, nomads,
in the desert. They traveled with their flock, tending to their
sheep and goats, and all their cooking used meat and dairy.
Mostly I hated milk. I refused to drink it, to the point where
it affected my teeth. But when Jadati cooked with milk, it
somehow always tasted delicious.

When my father was born, my grandparents gave up the
nomadic life and settled in Dara'a, a province in the southwest

corner of Syria. They built a house in the small town of Izraa, where our family has lived since. After Jidi died, Jadati moved in with us, which was really helpful, especially after my mom moved out.

Mohammed and I washed our hands and joined the others in one of the sitting rooms. The thin mattresses placed directly on the floor were great for jumping, flipping, and wrestling. The big pillows were perfect for reclining. They were also good for throwing, as necessary. If we were at home, this is where you'd find us.

Dad sat cross-legged on the mat, where we ate our meals together. My four-year-old brother, Zain, leaned on him from one side, and my eight-year-old sister, Yousra, leaned on him from the other. Jadati placed the steaming bowl of stew in the center of the mat. We each took a spoon and dug in.

"How was school today?" Dad asked.

Mohammed shrugged. He wasn't very interested in school.

"I have a story from English class," I offered, tearing a piece off a round, flat bread and dipping it into the stew. "Miss Leila said everyone who didn't do their homework must go out into the hallway and wait. So a few other students and I went into the hallway."

Jadati and Dad looked at me in dismay.

"Then Miss Leila went from desk to desk, asking students to read some text. She wanted to make sure they understood the lesson. She kept asking them to translate the term *al-bitriq tayir* into English. But no one she asked could do it."

I saw on Dad's face that he guessed where the story was going.

"So from the hallway, I called out the answer: 'Penguin!' And Miss Leila said, 'Muzoon, please go back to your seat.'"

Dad helped Zain spoon out a dumpling. "It's fine to be smart and resourceful," he began.

I blushed.

"But it's better to do your homework," he finished.

I thought he'd be pleased that I got the right answer. But Dad did not seem impressed.

"Remember when you were a preschooler?" Dad asked. I knew where *he* was going, because he told this story all the time. When I was just four years old, Aunt Zihriya, one of Dad's sisters, was the principal of an elementary school and would sometimes take me to work with her. They let me sit in on the first-grade class. I was what they called a "listener student." I didn't go every day and didn't do any assignments. But at the end of the year, the teacher gave me a diploma and a report card.

"Congratulations—you got top grades!" Aunt Zihriya beamed at me.

I got really angry and refused to accept the certificate. "I didn't earn this and I don't want it," I said, stomping.

"Who gets full marks and gets mad?" Aunt Zihriya asked in surprise.

"Me!"

Dad retold the story so many times that we could never forget it. He'd bring it up at just the right moment to make a point.

"Real success is earned through hard work," he said. And he turned his head to lock eyes with each of his four children, one at a time.

I helped Jadati clear the plates and got to work washing the dishes. I liked to do them, actually. We sometimes teased Jadati because she didn't use enough water. The dishes stayed soapy and we'd have to rinse them again.

"You kids don't appreciate the value of water!" she'd respond, her Bedouin accent getting stronger. "When I was young, we had to walk for hours to the well to fill each bucket. And our prophet Mohammed, peace be upon him, tells us to conserve water even if you live on the bank of a running stream." I tried not to waste water, but I loved the feel of hot water spilling over my hands.

When I finished, I found Mohammed back in the sitting room, ready for our afternoon dosage of cartoons. Razi knocked on the back door to join us. His siblings were older, so he loved to hang out with Mohammed and me. Sometimes he'd sneak out at night and cross through the groves to our house. Aunt Fadiya was very protective of him, though, so it wasn't long before she'd come over and drag him back.

"Is it time yet?" Razi asked excitedly.

We still had fifteen minutes—and they seemed like the longest minutes of our day. When it was finally time, I flipped on the TV and the three of us jumped to our feet and sang in unison.

"Ta ta tata ta, Majed!
Ta ta tata ta, Majed!

Ta ta tata ta, Majed has come back to you again,
Passing and assisting, he's ready to pay any price."

The theme song flowed into the show. We went silent in suspense and anticipation.

"I hope he scores this time," Razi whispered.

"Shhhhh!" we quieted him.

Every kid in Syria was where we were at that moment: spellbound by the same Japanese cartoon, dubbed in Arabic. Captain Majed was a soccer hero. He did legendary kicks, including somersaults and flips that revealed the number 10 on his back. Like us, he was determined to win. Unlike us, he never cheated. Instead, he learned a lesson from every defeat. He inspired his friends and made friends of his rivals. We all tried to do his tricks, but that resulted in accidents and injuries. It was not easy to match the moves of a cartoon champion.

When the episode finished, we went out again. Mansour and Tayyim met us in the street.

"I can't believe that Goalkeeper Waleed blocked Majed's scissors kick," Mansour said.

"I bet you can't block mine," I said.

I grabbed the ball, and our game picked up where we had left off. We played until we were so tired that we could hardly run anymore. But when our parents called us inside, we insisted that we were just getting started.

—

In the evening, we'd gather on the roof of our house. This was our favorite place. Uncle Adnan was there with Aunt Ayida. Aunt Fadiya was there with my cousins. The adults arranged mats in a circle around the tea and snacks.

We kids started a game of persis, which I'd later learn was like tic-tac-toe. I drew a grid on the cement floor with chalk, and each person got three whitish rocks and three dark ones. There are two players at a time. Each player would place one rock in the grid and take turns until someone made a line of six rocks of the same color.

Whoever was not playing watched from the sidelines. According to our rules, spectators were supposed to keep quiet. In practice, they whispered instructions, encouragement, and warnings as they wished. Struggling with the spectators became part of the game.

I won the first round against Mohammed, so I got to keep going against Yousra and then Razi, who defeated me in an extended play. So then I got up and wiped away the chalk that had somehow gotten all over my elbows and knees. I skipped back to the tray of snacks and stuffed a handful of sunflower seeds into my mouth. As I chewed, I listened in on the adults' conversation.

"Has Qutayba had any more luck finding work?" Uncle Adnan asked his sister. Aunt Fadiya shook her head. Razi's oldest brother had graduated from university, but he couldn't find stable employment in his field. He was doing odd jobs in construction to earn whatever he could.

"There's not much he can do without *wasta*," Uncle Adnan said sympathetically. Adults were always talking about *wasta*. They talked about it like it was more valuable than gold or diamonds. It took me years of eavesdropping before I understood that *wasta* meant having a relative or friend in some important position. Connections, they'd call it. From what they said, you couldn't get a job without *wasta* or open a store without *wasta*. People with *wasta* always seemed to be getting more than they deserved. People without *wasta* got less.

It was the same old conversation, so I went back to persis. We kept playing until it got so late that Yousra and Zain's eyes were closing. They went downstairs to go to sleep. Our relatives said their good-nights, and all went their separate ways.

Dad nodded toward the stairs. "Time for sleep, you two," he told Mohammed and me.

"Can we sleep on the roof? Tomorrow's Friday and there's no school."

"But tomorrow's the big harvest day. You need a good night's sleep."

"We'll sleep!"

"It's dangerous. There are some parts with no railing."

"Please! We want to count the stars."

"If you sleepwalk, you'll fall off."

"We promise that we won't walk," Mohammed said.

"How can you promise what you'll do while you sleep?"

Dad had a point, but we kept insisting. Eventually he gave in. We dragged mattresses up the stairs and placed them on the concrete floor. We got under layers of blankets and lay on our backs.

"Let's see who can count fifty stars the fastest," I told Mohammed.

The first thirty were always easy. After that, you had to be creative about where you searched the sky.

I don't remember how far I got. All I know is that I woke up on a mattress in the sitting room. Dad must have waited for us to fall asleep and then carried us down from the roof to keep us safe.

Chapter 3

By the time I woke up, Dad was already laying out mats under the olive trees.

Harvest day!

I wrapped my hands around the lowest branch of a tree and put one foot against its trunk. Then I pulled with my arms and swung my leg up and over the branch. I wrapped my legs to secure my position and scanned the branches. They were covered with finger-shaped leaves. I saw leaf after leaf, then spotted a flash of lighter green. I stretched out and plucked it from the branch. The olive dropped to the mat below with a light *pat.*

Abu Faysal's face came level with mine. "You know, it's easier with a ladder," he teased. "Then you can use your energy for picking instead of climbing."

Abu Faysal was Dad's best friend, and he joined us every October for the last big day of the olive harvest. Every relative who was able came to help that day. With all the family together, it felt like a holiday. Only Uncle Adnan's family was missing, because they had their hands full harvesting their own trees.

I lived much of my life in and around our olive, almond, and orange trees. In the summer we escaped the heat by having our meals in the shade of the grove. In the spring I studied for exams surrounded by new buds. I'd pace back and forth, barefoot in the grass, memorizing history or poetry. All year long, I swung on the swing that hung from one of the tallest branches. It had taken a long campaign to convince Dad to get a swing, but it was worth the wait.

Each season, our trees gave us something special. But autumn, and the olive harvest, was the most important of all.

From my place in the branches, I eyed another olive. I stretched long and plucked. Another green fruit fell to the mat with a small *pat.* It sounded like a raindrop. Abu Faysal and a few of Dad's cousins were atop ladders. When several of their olives fell to the mat at once, it sounded like the rain was getting stronger. Dad stood on the ground and ran a rake through the branches, shaking dozens of olives to the ground at a time. Those sounded like a storm. Dad's cousin Abu Mustafa used a rod and whacked down large bunches at once. That sounded like a sudden clap of thunder.

Mohammed was a climber, too. We'd pick and climb until the branches were bare. Yousra's job was to watch over Zain. Jadati served tea. Olive harvesting was hard work, and everyone had a role to play.

Pluck, pat. Pluck, pat. I sank into the rhythm of the work. Others' voices faded as I lost myself in daydreams or repeated to myself the poem that we were supposed to memorize for

Arabic class. Then a voice or a laugh would bring me back to the moment.

Pluck, pat. Pluck, pat. On and on, olive by olive, tree by tree.

Our work wound down along with the sun. Olives, leaves, and small branches lay in drifts on the mats. Mohammed and I took charge of scooping the olives into crates. It's easier to do when you're small. Abu Faysal pulled the heavy plastic mats to the open field and used his strength to fold them up. He always volunteered for the toughest task.

Harvesting olives was a lot of work, but these trees were ours, and with care and effort they earned us money. Dad's job as a teacher didn't pay enough to cover us the whole month. It was the same for most Syrians, especially if they worked for the government. Lots of people had to take second jobs to make ends meet. Some people couldn't find jobs at all and traveled far away to work in richer Arab countries, like Saudi Arabia or the United Arab Emirates. They'd send money home to their families.

Olives gave us the extra money that we needed to get by. We saved some olives for eating ourselves and took the rest to a big machine in town that pressed them into oil. People knew that if they wanted to buy oil, they could come and get it from us at home.

We washed up and ended harvest day with a big party. Jadati brought out heaping plates of the stuffed zucchini and stuffed grape leaves that she had been preparing all week. We passed around kibbeh—ground beef that was mixed with bulgur wheat, onions, and spices and then fried into perfect ovals. There was soda and fruit for all.

"My arms are so tired, I can barely lift my glass," Mohammed said.

I shrugged. "No problem—more cola for me." My arms were really sore, too, but in a satisfying way. I looked at the full crates and felt happy with what we had accomplished together.

Adults and kids sat under the trees and talked or sang. Neighbors and other relatives came by, too. When Aunt Zihriya arrived with a big plate of cookies to add to the feast, I greeted her with a huge hug.

"We'll go to my place and make more sweets tomorrow," she told me. She gave me a wink, as if it were our secret.

Aunt Zihriya's apartment was near downtown Izraa. It was only about a fifteen-minute drive or a thirty-minute bike ride from our house, but it felt farther. It was a modern apartment, with shiny new appliances and fancy furniture. There were no cousins or neighbor kids running in and out, like at our house. The streets were busy outside, but in the apartment, everything was tidy and peaceful—even the air felt calmer within her walls.

Aunt Zihriya lived with us in our house until I was seven. When she moved to her own place, I would often go stay with her on weekends. During the summers, I might spend whole weeks with her, returning to my own house only for visits. Aunt Zihriya and I had always been really close. After Mom moved out, we became closer still.

For as long as I could remember, my mom and dad were always arguing. Whatever the issue, they never saw eye to eye. They would get into fights, and Mom would leave for her parents' house. She'd stay away for a few days or weeks. Mohammed, Yousra, Zain, and I stayed with Dad. Sometimes we talked to Mom on the phone. Then she and Dad would reconcile, and she'd come back home.

When I was ten, their arguments started getting worse and lasting longer. Then Mom went away and stayed away. It was really hard at first. Jadati and Aunt Zihriya helped a lot, and our family adapted. I missed my mom but not the fighting. What bothered me most was the nosiness of other people. Some kids in school would ask where my mom was and why. Some ladies looked at me with pity, as if my family were somehow lesser. As if something were wrong with us or with me. I hated that.

But I didn't have to worry about any of that when I was with Aunt Zihriya. We'd take walks, go shopping, and stay up late watching TV. We got hooked on an Indian soap opera about Lakshmi Bai, a feisty and determined queen who was an expert swordfighter and led rebel forces against British colonialism. Our other favorite thing was taking notes during the *Manal Al-Alem's Kitchen* cooking show and re-creating the recipes.

On the screen, Manal wore a pink headscarf and matching pink apron. "This is one of the most beloved cakes in our region," Manal said. "It's a treat during Easter or Ramadan, or any time of the year."

"You're right, Manal." I spoke back to the TV set.

"In Egypt, they call it *basbousa*. In Lebanon, they call it *nammoura*. And in Syria they call it—"

"*Harissa!*" I cried.

"*Harissa,*" Manal said.

I punched my hands in the air, Captain Majed style.

"Okay," Aunt Zihriya said, calling me to the kitchen counter. "Two cups of semolina flour."

I dipped the cup into the tin and moved it to the mixing bowl. Aunt Zihriya blocked me with her hand.

"No need to rush," she said. I filled the cup again and this time used a knife to level it. Aunt Zihriya smiled approvingly.

"Now, one cup coconut flakes."

I measured that, too.

There was something about Aunt Zihriya that inspired you to try to do your best.

I know the students and staff in her school felt the same, and when we were out walking in town, many people would come and greet her by name. She had a unique kind of confidence, and just being with her made you feel more confident as well.

We added sugar and melted butter to the batter. I gave Aunt Zihriya a grin of anticipation. She nodded, and I dove in for the fun part: mixing it together with my hands. Aunt Zihriya poured in yogurt and baking soda from another bowl. I used my hands to mix that, too. Then I patted it into a baking dish. Aunt Zihriya cut the cake into a diamond pattern, and I pressed an almond into the middle of each piece.

We popped it into the oven to bake. As we waited, we made a syrup of sugar, water, and rose water.

Aunt Zihriya and I waited forty minutes and took the cake out of the oven. I could hardly wait to pour on the syrup and let it cool so I could try a piece. But when I finally did, it was terrible! It was crunchy when it should have been moist.

"How long did Manal say we should bake it?" I asked.

"I think we missed that part," Aunt Zihriya said, checking our notes. "But I think she did warn us to be careful not to overcook."

The disappointment must have shown on my face. Aunt Zihriya put her hand on my shoulder and whispered, "How about we go for a walk to get ice cream instead?" Even when things went wrong, she could make it right.

Chapter 4

It had been such a full weekend that Sunday morning, the first day of the school week, came as a shock.

"You're going to be late!" Jadati shook me awake.

I was not in the mood for getting out of bed. "I'm so tired. Can I skip today?" I asked.

Jadati raised her eyebrows in a way that ended discussions before they began. "Do you know how lucky you are? If I'd had the chance to go to school . . ."

Jadati was always saying things like this. When we threw away some unimportant worksheet from school, she would rescue it from the wastebasket and flatten it smooth. "You should keep this," she'd say, returning it to us. "If your grandfather were alive, he would want you to save every paper."

Jidi had grown up an orphan and never learned to read and write. Back then only a few people went to school. And no girls went to school at all. But when Jidi and Jadati got married, their first children were girls. Jidi wanted to educate them even before their brothers came along.

"Why bother? A girl is only going to get married," people objected.

But Jidi insisted.

Dad's oldest sister, Aunt Fatima, was the first girl to go to school in all of Izraa. She didn't complete her education, but my aunts Zihriya, Fadiya, and Yousra all did. Then Dad and my uncles Adnan and Mohammed followed their sisters' example. Mohammed and Yousra died before I was born. Fadiya, Adnan, and Dad all became schoolteachers. And Zihriya was a teacher before she became a principal.

Everyone in the community believed that girls were supposed to get married young and have children. But Jidi had different views on this, too. He told his daughters that marriage was their choice. They could decide whom they wanted to marry and when. Or they could decide not to marry at all. That was Aunt Zihriya's choice. She had her own job, apartment, and car, and she liked her independent life. "You can choose your own path," she'd tell me when we stayed up late at her place. "But you can't do *anything* without an education."

In my family, school meant everything.

I pulled on my school uniform—pants, jacket, pink shirt—and chose a white hijab. I felt proud when I started wearing it at the beginning of seventh grade. It was a sign that I was growing up. Most days I wore the ready-made hijab, which was made of a stretchy material like a T-shirt. It was snug around my face like a very wide headband and then draped over my head to my shoulders. The ready-made was great for sports and climbing trees. And I didn't usually have the patience to wrap a scarf properly and pin it in all the right places.

Yousra and Mohammed were still in the elementary school, so they went off in that direction. I headed to the middle school, noting all of the landmarks on my route. I started under the canopy of grape leaves and vines that grew outside my front door, then cut around the back of the house and through our fields till I reached the main street. From there I headed down the hill to Nayef's store. That was where we kids spent any money we got our hands on. Nayef had all types of candy and chips in addition to all the basic things families needed for cooking. He didn't have ice cream, though. For ice cream, you had to walk to a store twice as far away.

Nayef's store was a major landmark for our neighborhood. Streets didn't have names and houses didn't have numbers, so to tell someone how to get to our house, we'd say, "Up the street from Nayef's store, with the grapevines out front."

Most of the families in our neighborhood were Muslim. And past the narrow road with lemon trees, most of the families were Christian. Most of my classmates were Christian, too. So was Abu Faysal, Dad's best friend. Sometimes you knew who was from which religion and sometimes you didn't. We didn't ask, and it wasn't something we thought much about unless somebody wanted to get married outside of their religion.

Aside from Nayef's store, the other marker in our

neighborhood was the huge military base. We didn't think much about that, either. It was less than a mile away and towered above the houses. We were used to seeing people in uniform around town.

I arrived at the gates of the school and joined the lines forming for morning assembly. The seventh, eighth, and ninth grades each separated into groups A, B, and C. I found my place in Seven B. Each group formed a very straight line facing the school principal.

The principal called us to order.

"Attention!" he shouted. Everyone pressed their hands to their sides and stood up as straight as they could.

"At ease," he said. We let our posture relax and stepped one leg out to the right.

"Attention!" he shouted again. We again stood tall.

He then led us in the national motto. "One Arab Nation!" he called.

"One Eternal Message!" we chanted in unison.

"Our Goals," he called.

"Unity, Freedom, Socialism!" we responded.

We had been shouting the motto every morning since first grade. I knew it as well as I did my own name, though I never thought much about what it meant.

The principal continued. "My dear vanguard youth, are you ready to build one Arab nation?" he asked.

"We are ready!" we responded.

He then raised the flag and we sang the national anthem.

We pinned our eyes on the flag. But from the corner of my eye I saw a flash of blue uniform. A boy was arriving late. My heart pounded for him. He was going to get in big trouble. I tried to follow him without moving my eyes. I didn't want to get in trouble, too. I sensed the boy trying to slip into the Eight C line, hoping no one would notice. The vice-principal caught him. My heart pounded harder. He was going to get hit.

"Your generation has it easy," Dad always reminded us. When he was in school, they had to wear khaki uniforms and black boots. It was like they were in the army. Each grade had a different set of military stripes on the left shoulder. They had a military training class, where they learned how to shoot guns. The military training teachers were famous for screaming and beating kids who didn't follow orders correctly. Trainers had more power than regular teachers. They could punish any student they wished.

By the time I was in school, it had become a less scary place. They got rid of the military uniforms and the military training class. They told teachers that they couldn't beat kids or make them crawl around the schoolyard on their hands and knees as punishment. Instead, teachers would hit students on the hand with a stick. Sometimes teachers would appoint a student to keep track of other kids who were misbehaving. The appointed student would write names on the board, and then teachers would call those students from their desks. One by one, they would stretch out their hands and wait.

I took my seat in the front of the class. Our classroom had three rows of desks. Three students sat at each desk. We didn't have assigned seats. On the first day of school, you grabbed the seat you wanted, and it would be yours for the year. Bad students sat in the back rows, where they hoped teachers would ignore them. I sat in the front because I didn't like to be ignored. I wasn't the best student, but was never shy to raise my hand.

I shared my desk with Jamila and Hanin. At another desk in the front row sat Reem, the best student in class. When old ladies wanted to praise girls, they would say that they were calm and quiet. Reem was calm and quiet, so adults loved her. I was not calm or quiet, but I liked Reem a lot, too.

Reem always sat next to her best friend, Fadia. Behind me sat Malak and Jamella. They were also calm and quiet. My deskmate Jamila was especially smart but had very bad handwriting, just like I did. Sometimes teachers gave her bad marks on exams simply because they could not understand anything she'd written.

The day passed slowly: French, English, geography, math, biology, chemistry, physics, history, Arabic.

In history, we reviewed what Miss Hadeel had told us last week about World War I. Before the war, most Arab people were subjects of the Ottoman Empire, which was ruled by a Turkish sultan in Istanbul. After the war, the Ottoman Empire collapsed and European countries took control of Arab lands.

"What was the Sykes-Picot Agreement?" Miss Hadeel asked.

I got my hand in the air before Reem did. "Sykes was British and Picot was French. They got together and drew borders that created new countries like Syria, Lebanon, Jordan, and Iraq."

"Very good. Why did they do that?"

This time Reem got her hand in the air first.

"It was an imperialist conspiracy to divide the unified Arab nation," she said. Reem was very good at using the exact words from the textbook.

"Correct." Miss Hadeel nodded. "Britain ruled some Arab countries and France ruled others. France ruled Syria until our revolution triumphed and Syria won its independence in 1946."

I really liked history class, but it left me with so many questions. Other Arab countries got independence from colonial powers around the time Syria did. So why did we still have the borders that were placed on us? We learned that our goal was to be unified with the rest of the Arab world. So why did we remain divided?

We also learned about more recent history. Hafez al-Assad became our president in 1971. There was a huge statue of him downtown. His picture was on our textbooks, report cards, and notebooks. If you ever marked on that picture by mistake, you'd be in big trouble. We memorized his sayings. Teachers cited his accomplishments throughout the school day, even in math class. Our book referred to him as "The Immortal Leader," though he had died when I was two. Then his son, Bashar al-Assad, became president. Portraits of both father and son hung in school classrooms and hallways. They hung in many other places, too.

The walls had a lot of eyes. And Dad told us that the walls might have ears as well. So I saved my questions for home.

School was a place where the teacher told us answers and we memorized them.

Not that I minded memorizing. You could do it while walking between trees. I especially liked memorizing Arabic poetry. Dad loved poetry, and I inherited that from him.

When history class ended and it was time for Arabic, I was ready to go.

"Last week we talked about a Tunisian poet," Miss Hadeel said. "Your homework was to memorize—"

My hand was in the air before she could even ask for a volunteer.

"Muzoon, would you like to recite it?"

Within seconds, I was on my feet. I turned toward the class and recited with confidence.

" 'If the People Wanted Life One Day' by Abu al-Qassim al-Shabbi.

> *"If, one day, a people desires to live, then fate will answer*
>   *their call.*
> *And their night will then begin to fade, and their chains*
>   *break and fall.*
> *For he who is not embraced by a passion for life will*
>   *dissipate into thin air,*
> *At least that is what all creation has told me, and what*
>   *its hidden spirits declare."*

I liked lots of poems, but this one stood out. It felt like a personal message, like Abu al-Qassim al-Shabbi was reading my thoughts and giving me encouragement. It was like he was telling me, "You can do it, Muzoon. Set a goal and never give up." His words gave me power. No wonder I had turned them over and over again in my mind while picking olives last weekend.

PART II

REVOLUTION

January 2011

*The spring of 2011 brought an unexpected kind
of renewal. There was change in the air. Hope.
Excitement. And danger.*

Chapter 5

I remember that Aunt Zihriya and I made a chocolate cake with sparkle frosting for New Year's Eve. We stayed up until the clock struck midnight, and then we shouted out, "Two thousand eleven!"

I remember racing my classmates inside school to gather around the gas heater, each of us trying to get closest to the flame.

But the best part of winter was hunting for mushrooms.

"I found one!" I squealed. Mohammed ran over and had to admit I'd found a good one.

We'd spent the whole morning out in the fields, looking everywhere a mushroom might hide. I scanned the horizon one last time. "Let's go in," I said.

We wiped the mud off our shoes, unwrapped our winter layers, and went to the sitting room. There we found Jadati and Dad, glued to the news. That was weird. Dad had gone with Uncle Adnan to the mosque for Friday noon prayers. He normally didn't get home this early.

As Muslims, we pray five times a day. You could pray anywhere, but on Fridays, men usually went to the mosque at midday to pray together.

Jadati had taught me how to pray, which I did at home. First you perform *wudu*—washing yourself before prayers. Then you stand at the top of your prayer rug, raise your hands to either side of your head, fold your hands over your chest, and raise them again. You bow, stand up, kneel to put your forehead to the ground, rise to a sitting position, prostrate again, stand again, and repeat. You recite *surah Al-Fatiha* and other verses from the Quran. It is a time to praise God, to ask for guidance or forgiveness. When Mohammed and I were little, we used to climb on top of Jadati's back when she prostrated in prayer. She would show no reaction as she concentrated on her recitations. When she finished, she'd chase after us. We'd bolt out the door and sometimes up a tree.

After Friday prayers at the mosque, Dad and Uncle Adnan would sometimes stop at a coffee shop. But today he must have rushed right home.

"What's going on?" I asked.

He motioned toward the television, where Al Jazeera was on. Al Jazeera is an international satellite channel where we always went for news, specifically to find out what was happening in Syria. Syrian channels didn't tell us much.

The screen showed thousands of people marching down a tree-lined boulevard. There were bodies as far as the eye could see. Some people were carrying loaves of bread. Many held signs. The camera zoomed in on a few of them. They had messages like "Freedom" and "Game Over."

"Where is this?" I asked.

"Tunisia," Dad said.

The crowd seemed angry and joyous at the same time. They were chanting something, but I couldn't make it out exactly. It sounded like "Garage! Garage!"

"What's happening in the garage?" I asked.

Dad looked at me like I was crazy.

"They keep shouting 'Garage.'"

Dad burst out laughing. "They're saying *'Dégage.'*" He clarified. "It's French, for 'Leave' or 'Get lost.'"

That did not make me any less confused.

"People are on the streets demanding that the president step down," Dad explained.

I'd never heard of anything like that before. No wonder there was a special broadcast. I grabbed a pillow and settled in on the mattress.

"The president has kept an iron grip on power there for more than twenty-three years," Dad continued. "The Tunisian people are fed up. They want real elections so they can choose new leaders, and make sure those leaders serve the people, not just themselves. They want to be able to criticize the government without being afraid that the police will throw them in jail. They want to be free."

Over the next many hours, we hardly moved from the TV. Jadati brought in lunch, and our eyes stayed glued as we ate. Yousra followed along, even though she was too little to understand much. The news commentators filled us in on the background. In a small Tunisian town not that different from mine, a young man named Mohammed Bouazizi was selling fruits and vegetables from a cart on the street. He didn't have a permit to sell things, but he couldn't find any other work. A city employee saw him and confiscated his weighing scales. Some said that she also insulted him, or that the police came and beat him.

Bouazizi went to the governor's office to ask for his scales back. The officials refused to meet with him. He'd had similar problems before. This time, he'd had enough. He got a can of gasoline and poured it over himself, right there in the middle of the street.

"And then what happened?" I asked.

"He lit himself on fire," Dad said.

"*What?*" I gasped. I couldn't imagine anything so terrible. "Why would he do a thing like that?"

"I guess he'd taken all the humiliation he could, and he couldn't stand it anymore," Dad said. "People say that the last thing he shouted was 'How do you expect me to make a living?'"

I was horrified. It was unbelievable.

But I thought about my cousins and all the other young people I knew who were desperate to find jobs. I thought about the people I'd heard of who'd been insulted by police or slapped by security force officers. It was unbelievable, and also familiar. The more details I heard on the news, the more Tunisia sounded like Syria.

After Bouazizi died, others in his town went out in

protest. During the weeks that followed, protests spread from one town to another. People marched in the streets and called for justice and change. Police shot them with bullets or beat them with clubs. The protests got bigger.

"Dictators think that violence will make people too afraid to speak out." Dad shook his head. "But it only makes them more angry and determined."

The protests in Tunisia had been going on for about a month when activists called for a huge demonstration in the capital. That was what we were watching on our TV screen. About ten thousand people marched in the center of the city. Their chants and demands expressed things that many Syrians held in their hearts but didn't say out loud. It seemed like the Tunisians hadn't dared to say them out loud before, either. But now they were saying, "Enough." Enough of corruption and injustice. We want to be treated with dignity.

One man turned to the camera, and his words conveyed it all: "The barrier of fear has broken," he said.

The news continued until evening, and we hardly moved from the TV. At one point, Mohammed interrupted the rapt stillness in the room.

"*Captain Majed* is starting—can we change the channel?" he asked.

"This is not a time for cartoons—something important is happening," Dad said without turning from the screen.

"*Captain Majed* is important," Mohammed mumbled under his breath. I elbowed him to shut up. I was captivated by what I saw unfolding. I felt excited and proud that Tunisians were doing what I had never imagined was possible. I felt scared for them, too. The strange thing was that I seemed more afraid than the protesters themselves. They were brave and filled with energy.

Finally it was getting to be time to go to sleep. I left the TV to get ready for bed. I was brushing my teeth when Dad called out from the sitting room, "Tunisia's president stepped down. He fled the country. The people won!"

Chapter 6

The next day was Saturday. Mohammed and I met our cousins in the street to play soccer, as we did every day there wasn't school. But there was something different in the air. I couldn't quite put my finger on it, but I felt it.

I was bursting with excitement to talk about what had happened in Tunisia. Still, everyone was cautious. We knew that you shouldn't talk about politics. But was something shifting here, too?

I overheard two neighbors near the brick wall where we practiced shooting soccer goals. Abu Yousef and Abu Ahmed stopped and chatted. I pretended to play as I got close enough to listen to their conversation.

"*As-salamu alaykum.* Peace be upon you."

"*Wa alaykumu s-salam.* And upon you peace."

"How are you today, Abu Ahmed?"

"Good, thanks be to God. How are you, Abu Yousef?"

"Very good."

"Very good?"

"Yes, by God, very good."

"Yes, I'm very good. Excellent, really. Thanks be to God."

"It's a beautiful day today."

"Yes indeed, it's extraordinarily beautiful. Thanks be to God."

It might seem like a normal conversation. But I could tell that the real message lay between the words. It was like they were each trying to say, "Can you believe what happened in Tunisia? Do you think it could happen here, too?"

We played soccer and then got bored and rode bikes. We got bored with that, broke for lunch, and then restarted our soccer game. When we got bored with that, we played *Valley of the Wolves*, based on the Turkish soap opera that was becoming our passion. It was dubbed in Arabic with a Damascus accent and featured a detective named Murad. He used ingenious ways to catch mafia bosses. My cousins and Mohammed and I would reenact the scenes, running between the trees and pointing plastic water guns in every direction. The problem was that we each wanted to play Murad. We would argue about it and then eventually agree that all of us could be Murad and we would just imagine the criminals.

By evening, it was time for the real Murad. We cousins parted ways and headed to our TV sets. When Mohammed and I got to the sitting room, we found Dad watching Al Jazeera again.

"Can we switch to Murad?"

"No, this is important."

"But Murad is in the middle of a fierce debate with the chief of police."

"If you kids want debate, then this is the show for you. It's called *The Opposite Opinion*."

"Huh?"

"Two guests with different points of view debate a theme. The host moderates."

I sat down. That could be interesting.

The first guest began with a speech about security and stability. He talked about the need to keep order and praised governments in Arab countries for having strong leaders.

The other guest shook his head in disagreement. "Our leaders are dictators who oppress their own people," he shouted. "But the Tunisian people refuse to be oppressed any longer. They are living the words of their homeland's great poet Abu al-Qassim al-Shabbi. . . ."

My eyes widened. The guest began reciting, and I jumped to my feet and said every word in harmony with him:

"If one day, a people desires to live, then fate will answer their call.
And their night will then begin to fade, and their chains break and fall."

Dad gave me a teasing ovation. I sat down, pleased with my performance.

"A truly political poem," Dad said with a grin.

"What do you mean?" I asked.

"Think about the words," Dad said.

I rolled them over in my mind again. Not just memorizing them, as I had done before, but really thinking about the meaning. And it hit me that Miss Hadeel hadn't explained the full meaning of the poem. And I hadn't grasped it myself, either. I'd thought it was about personal ambition, but now I saw it was about something much bigger. It was about an entire people wanting better lives. It was about people realizing that they have the power to demand freedom.

The days passed as they usually did: school, playing, homework, helping Jadati with Zain and Yousra before Dad came home, soccer and TV after that. I spent a few nights at Aunt Zihriya's.

I was spread out on the sitting room floor doing my math homework one afternoon when Dad came bursting through the door.

"You're here early!" I said as I met him with a hug. "Is everything okay?"

"Egypt," he replied, clicking on the TV.

We all gathered and watched the breaking news flash. "We're broadcasting live from Tahrir Square in downtown Cairo," the reporter said, surrounded by a sea of people. "Inspired by Tunisia, an estimated twenty thousand Egyptians are out on the streets to demand the resignation of President Hosni Mubarak, who has ruled Egypt for nearly thirty years."

Egypt! Now *this* was news. The resignation of Tunisia's

president eleven days earlier was exciting. But Tunisia was a small country, and it didn't play a large role in the Middle East. Egypt was a different story. Any Syrian kid who passed elementary school geography could tell you that it was the largest Arab country, in terms of population anyway. We all grew up watching Egyptian movies and listening to Egyptian music. Egyptians referred to their country as *Um al-Dunya*, Mother of the World. Anything that happened there was a big deal.

We lost ourselves in the news broadcast. Men, women, even kids marched and chanted. The crowds insisted on making it to Tahrir Square. It wasn't lost on us that *tahrir* means "liberation" in Arabic. Police tried to block their way by attacking the crowds with tear gas and water cannons. But people didn't run away. Some even shouted at the police. They looked very brave, joyful even. "This is the happiest day of my life," a young woman told a reporter. A man looked into the camera and said, "The people want the overthrow of the regime!"

"What's a regime?" I asked.

Dad paused. "It's like the government, but more specific," he said. "It's the group that rules over people."

Day became evening and the protesters occupied Tahrir Square. It was like a movie—we watched and ate popcorn, enthralled.

If the start of the Egyptian revolution was like a movie, the next days offered sequels no less dramatic. I rushed home from school to see the news. I took the shortcut through the rocky field, even though it left my school shoes covered in dust.

At home, I went straight to the sitting room and clicked on the broadcast live from Cairo. Thousands of people of different backgrounds were still occupying Tahrir Square, refusing to leave until the president resigned. They slept in tents and set up their own clinics. They cleaned the streets, ate together, and made new friendships. The police used violence to force them out, and many people got killed or injured, but thousands remained. The army brought out tanks and soldiers, but the soldiers refused to shoot and the crowds cheered them.

Once, Dad came home from work and was surprised to see me watching the news.

"Don't you feel like playing outside today?" he asked with a raised eyebrow.

"Not really," I said matter-of-factly. "I want to know what's happening."

"Hmm," he said, nodding in interest. "Would you rather change the channel to cartoons?"

I looked at him like he was crazy. "Cartoons? Dad, this is a revolution!"

"Indeed." He smiled.

It was strange to use the word "revolution." In history class we read about revolutions for independence against colonial powers. Now I realized that there could be revolutions against our current leaders. Regular people can start a revolution, and young people can even lead it. All the Egyptian flags that filled the square showed that the protesters loved their country. They were coming together to make it better for everyone.

After eighteen days of protests, the Egyptian president stepped down.

If, one day, a people desires to live, then fate will answer their call.

Chapter 7

The day after Egyptians forced their president to resign, the mood in our town was joyful. Rumors spread that Syrians in other cities were even giving out candy in the streets, like we do to celebrate a new birth. We started to hear about small protests in other Arab countries. In Yemen, Libya, and Bahrain, protesters began calling for the overthrow of their regimes. People started calling it the Arab Spring.

Where else would it spread? Could it happen in Syria, too? Even after everything I'd seen, I couldn't imagine that at all.

One of our neighbors, Abu Saloum, came by one night a few weeks later. I was in the sitting room doing my homework, and no one seemed to mind that I stayed there as they talked and drank their tea.

"Did you see on Facebook"—my father put an extra spoonful of sugar into his glass—"a policeman insulted and beat the son of one of the merchants in the marketplace in Damascus."

"So?" Abu Saloum asked, sipping his tea. "That happens all the time."

"But this time, hundreds of people gathered and started shouting at the officer."

Abu Saloum nearly spilled his tea on his lap.

Dad chuckled. "I wouldn't believe it myself if I hadn't seen the video." He scrolled on his phone and pressed play. Abu Saloum got closer to the phone's small screen and watched. No one seemed to notice when I did the same.

The video showed people as far as the eye could see. Many held up cell phones and were filming. "Thieves!" they shouted at the police. One man started chanting, "The Syrian people will not be humiliated!" The whole crowd repeated the chant: "The Syrian people will not be humiliated!"

Abu Saloum shook his head in disbelief. "This is really in Damascus? In the capital? I need to see it again," he said. Dad nodded and replayed it, then replayed it again. I switched back and forth between watching the video and watching Abu Saloum's face. He looked like he was seeing people fly.

"It might be just the beginning," Dad added. "The Facebook page is calling for protests to start all over Syria on March fifteenth."

I looked over at Abu Saloum and was surprised to see his eyes fill with tears. Dad wiped away tears, too.

—

Anticipation built for March fifteenth. And then the date came and went. The video we saw on Facebook that night showed a small demonstration in Damascus, with protesters chanting bravely. But the police were there in large numbers. The demonstration lasted only a few minutes before they started beating people. Some protesters managed to run away, but many were arrested.

"Our struggle finished before it even began," Dad said.

Mohammed and I went back to watching *Captain Majed*, but it didn't interest us as much as it used to. Thursday night I slept over at Aunt Zihriya's. The next day we were preparing an early lunch. She stirred the green bean stew. I chopped the cucumbers and tomatoes for salad.

"Very small pieces," she instructed me.

I cut the pieces a bit smaller. Then I added olive oil, mint, and lemon, and tossed.

We set the table and clicked on the TV. My back was turned to the screen when I heard the newscaster's voice: "A huge protest is happening in the city of Dara'a," she said.

I nearly dropped the salad. Dara'a was my province! Dara'a City, the provincial capital, was less than thirty minutes from Izraa by car. I'd bought my favorite dress there. We went there for all our official documents, or to meet up with a shared taxi that Mom would send for us whenever we visited her.

I never thought there would be protests so close to home. It made sense for them to be in the capital, Damascus. Aunt Zihriya had taken me on a trip there when I was eleven. It was so busy with people and cars. By comparison, Dara'a Province was mostly a farming area. Sometimes it seemed like the rest of the country forgot we were here.

"Crowds are chanting for freedom and dignity in the first mass demonstration of its kind in Syria."

I plopped down cross-legged on the couch, and Aunt Zihriya sat next to me. We saw images of huge crowds marching and clapping. One man sat atop another's shoulders, waving his arms to guide the chanting. Another man called through a megaphone and urged others to join. Two red fire trucks parked on a bridge blocked the protesters from crossing to the other side of town. As the march got closer, the trucks sprayed thick jets of water and charged in their direction.

The newscasters were explaining how the protest began. Twelve days earlier, teachers and students had arrived at school in Dara'a City to find a message spray-painted on the school wall: "It's your turn, Doctor."

I gasped when I heard that. It was obvious that this was a direct message to our president, who was an eye doctor. I could not even imagine seeing those words in public.

The school principal reported the graffiti to the intelligence services. Security agents came and arrested about fifteen students. Most were teenagers just a few years older than me. No one really knew who wrote the slogan, so these arrests seemed random.

Elders from the kids' families did what they could to get them released. They asked local officials for help but came away empty-handed. Then they made a formal visit to the chief of political security for Dara'a Province. The elders went to him with respect and deference, but he told them to get out and forget their children. And that was not all. He insulted them with an insult so horrible that when I heard it, my face turned bright red.

So that was what had led up to today. Many men went to pray at mosques, like on any other Friday. But some had a plan.

Prayers ended as they usually did. Then, suddenly, one young man jumped to his feet. He shouted, "God is great!" It was a signal to protest. A few of his friends were there, waiting for the signal. They leaped to their feet and also shouted, "God is great!"

Others immediately recognized what was going on. Some older men got scared. They ran as fast as they could to find their shoes at the door of the mosque. But many young people were determined. They chanted, "God! Syria! *Freedom! And that's it!*"

The demonstration moved into the streets and wound toward the center of town. Bystanders were amazed as they watched the clapping and chanting. Some people froze. More and more joined. The demonstration grew to hundreds and then thousands. It stopped at the edge of the valley that separated the residential part of the city from the part where government buildings were located. Security forces gathered on the other side. They pointed their guns at the crowd. And opened fire.

Several people were shot. Two young men died instantly. We watched all this happening, live on TV.

Aunt Zihriya and I watched until the green bean stew got cold and the cucumbers in the salad lost their crunch. I felt the strange mix of emotions that I'd felt while watching the protests in Tunisia and Egypt, but many times stronger. I felt pride and joy at seeing my people standing up against injustice. I felt deep sadness for those who were killed and for their families, who would mourn them forever. I felt angry that my government was killing us. Most of all, I felt shock that all this was happening just a few miles away from where I sat.

It was unthinkable. But I was watching it happen.

The next day, there was an enormous funeral for the two young men who had been killed. The news estimated that twenty thousand people gathered to mourn. That was as many as the entire population of Izraa. People started chanting, and the funeral became a protest. Protests continued for three days after that. And there were more deaths and injuries. Some injured protesters were holed up in Dara'a's biggest mosque. They were too afraid to go to a hospital. People said that security agents were going to hospitals and arresting people, viewing any injury as proof that you'd been protesting.

On Wednesday, security forces stormed the mosque. They killed five people inside, as well as a woman who lived nearby. The government cut electricity so that no one could communicate. But word still flew from friend to friend and relative to relative. Before long, all of Dara'a Province knew. In the surrounding villages, people got scared that there was going to be a massacre. They flocked to Dara'a City to help. People came in cars and on foot. They shouted, *"Fazza! Fazza!"* That is a special word that we use in Dara'a. It is a call to come to others' aid in time of need.

But as the helpers were approaching, the security forces opened fire. People from many different villages were killed. People had gone to stand with their neighbors. The government sent home martyrs across the region.

In Izraa, everyone traded information about what was happening. Dad flipped between channels trying to learn more. On one of the Syrian channels, the newscaster looked straight at the screen and said, "An armed gang attacked an ambulance in Dara'a."

"What?!" I exclaimed, jumping to my feet. Facebook and Al Jazeera had told a different story.

The camera flashed to a mountain of guns and other weapons. "Security forces uncovered weapons that armed gangs obtained from foreign sources."

I felt really angry. Those weren't armed gangs but innocent people, and they were being killed.

I wasn't the only one who was upset. I felt it in the air that afternoon when Tayyim, Razi, Mohammed, and I kicked the ball around in the streets. I felt it during the walk to Nayef's store when Jadati sent me with a list of vegetables to buy for dinner. And I felt it that Friday. It was exactly one week from the first big protest in Dara'a. Everybody wondered what would happen.

What happened was that the country erupted. There were protests *all over* Syria. Tens of thousands of people were saying that Dara'a's dreams for change were their dreams. Dara'a's dead were their dead. I felt our people come together. Syrians in the north and the south and the east and the west were united. I had never felt so close to every other person in my country.

But by the end of the day, many other towns were mourning dead of their own, too.

Chapter 8

March became April. The protest movement kept growing. People started calling it a revolution. Here! In Syria!

The demonstrations we watched on TV were the most beautiful things I had ever seen. People joined hands and sang and danced. It was like they tasted freedom for the first time in their lives. You could see the spirit of togetherness and caring.

And courage. So much courage! People knew they could be killed if they protested, but they did it anyway. When some were shot, others risked their lives and went into the gunfire to drag them to safety. Some people covered their faces to disguise themselves. Others bravely and defiantly showed theirs, even though the security forces would track them down and raid their homes. Activists started living on the run, moving from place to place or sleeping in the fields to avoid arrest.

My older cousins, Razi's brothers Qutayba and Mohammed, went to nearby towns to participate. So did Aghiad, Mansour and Tayyim's oldest brother. My uncles tried to prevent them. They said it was too dangerous. The regime sometimes arrested not only protesters but their family members as well. This was to frighten people and stop them from protesting in the first place. My cousins went out anyway. Hundreds of thousands of young people all over the country did the same. Everywhere, people were breaking through the barrier of fear. They called for freedom and dignity. They wanted to be able to speak their opinions without being afraid. They didn't want to have to pay bribes when they went to a government office. They wanted to be treated with respect. They wanted a Syria that was for all Syrians.

I lost interest in cartoons and became obsessed with the news. I was hungry to know everything: where demonstrations were happening and whether anyone was killed. The biggest demonstrations happened on Fridays, so protesters could use mosques as places to gather. Activists gave each Friday a special name: "Friday of Martyrs," "Friday of Persistence," "Friday of Rage," "Friday of Defiance" . . .

"Great Friday" was declared in honor of Easter, which was the following Sunday. It was a sign of respect for Syria's Christian population. It was a message that this was their revolution, too. People were expecting protests to be really large.

On that April day our fields smelled like springtime, which meant it was time to pick fresh green almonds. Before almonds ripen into a hard nut, they are white, squishy, and covered with a fuzzy green shell. Green almonds are more delicious than brown ones, if you ask me.

Every year, Mohammed and I filled buckets with green

almonds from our trees. Mansour and Tayyim did the same from their trees. We made it into a contest, as we did with everything. Each pair of siblings would go house to house, and whoever sold the most almonds won. We agreed on a fixed price in advance, so victory was measured not by money but by weight sold. The key to winning was your ability to convince people to buy. I loved that part.

Mohammed and I always defeated our cousins. To be honest, we had an advantage. The almonds from our trees were the sweet kind, which people liked more. Our uncle's trees bore bitter almonds, which attracted fewer customers. Still, I liked to think that my sales pitch was the reason for our success.

That Friday, Mohammed and I loaded up two buckets with almonds, caught a shared service taxi toward downtown, and chose a street to get started.

Knock, knock!

"*Meen?* Who is it?"

Mohammed went silent with nervous shyness, as he usually did when someone answered the door. His big eyelashes would follow his eyes down to his feet. But as he went silent, I found my voice. I would feel as powerful as I did when I was reciting poetry in front of the class.

"Sweet green almonds!" I sang out. "Fresh from the tree, only thirty lira a kilo."

A man came to the door. He bought a kilo.

First house was a sale! Mohammed and I high-fived as we walked away. A great start.

We moved on to the next house. I heard faint rumbles in the distance that grew steadily louder. Then the rumbles became chants. It was a demonstration! The crowd was still too far away to see. But the shouts were just like those we heard daily on TV.

Suddenly the sounds changed. A burst of heavy machine-gun fire ripped through the air. It was followed by pained wailing.

"What should we do?" Mohammed asked, his voice quivering.

My mind raced through our options. We should run away from the crowd. But we couldn't run if we were weighed down by two buckets of almonds. Our best option was to try to sell the rest of the almonds as quickly as we could.

We walked to the next house and knocked on the door. I peered through the window and managed to make out hushed whispers and blurred movements. No one answered.

"They probably think that we're security forces coming to arrest them," Mohammed said. His eyebrows knit with worry. "Do you think we'll get arrested?"

Without responding, I moved to the next house. This time the door opened slowly. A face peeked out from behind the door. First it was cautious. Then the eyes widened in shock. Finally they softened with laughter. "What a great time for selling almonds!" the woman said sarcastically. The door closed again.

Meanwhile, the sound of shooting had not stopped. I scanned the street and saw a shop on the corner.

"Let's try to hide," I told Mohammed.

We walked into the shop, which sold cylinders of gas to fuel space heaters and stoves.

"What are you kids doing outside?" the man at the counter asked. "I think you better get home."

For sure, home was where I wanted to be. Mohammed and I locked eyes. We both understood what we needed to do. We dropped our buckets of unsold almonds on the floor of the store and ran home as fast as we could.

When Dad came back that afternoon, he yelled at us like we had never been yelled at before. "Don't you realize you could have been killed?" His voice was about seventy-five percent anger and twenty-five percent relief.

That night we switched on state TV. Their news said that a protester had shot at the police and caused a riot. They said that police acted with restraint to quell the unrest.

Other channels told a different story. They insisted that ordinary citizens held a peaceful protest in front of the mayor's office. Hundreds of people marched toward a bridge that was closed by checkpoints on both ends. Security forces cleared one checkpoint and let them march through. Suddenly they set up the checkpoint again. The crowd was trapped. Guns pointed at them from in front and behind. Normally, demonstrators would have scattered to side streets as soon as security forces arrived. Stuck on the bridge, there was nowhere they could run.

That was when security forces opened fire. Some people

were shot and died instantly. Some were wounded, and they bled until the checkpoints opened and others managed to drag them away. Someone filmed the scene on a cell phone, and the video clip circulated on social media. Mohammed and I gathered around Dad's phone and watched. The clip began with a hail of gunfire.

"That's exactly what we heard!" Mohammed exclaimed.

I elbowed him to be quiet. He didn't need to make Dad more upset.

The clip continued. The camera jumped around un-steadily and then turned upside down. I tried to imagine the fear and panic of the person filming. Several people were on the ground, covered in blood. Some moaned in pain. Others were lifeless and made no sound at all. Those who were unwounded struggled to carry or drag away those who were. Shouts of shock were the main soundtrack.

"Peaceful! Peaceful! It's a peaceful demonstration," the people yelled out, over and over.

"Ambulance! We need an ambulance! Where's the ambulance?" others cried in desperation.

"My brother," wailed another voice.

Many, many voices called out to God.

More than a few times, I found myself squeezing my eyes shut to block out the terrible images. It was like a horror movie, but real. I called out to God, too.

We kept watching the news. "Huge demonstrations hap-pened all over Syria today," the newscaster said. "At least seventy-five people were killed, making today the bloodiest day of the monthlong uprising."

"Two weeks ago they said that was the bloodiest day," I replied to the TV set.

"It was," Dad said. "And now there is a new bloodiest day."

And it was here. In my town.

I went to bed very early that night because I wasn't in the mood for anything else. The next day there was a huge funeral procession in Izraa to honor those who had been killed. People came to participate from many neighboring towns, just like people from Izraa had gone to funerals in other towns. It was how we expressed solidarity with each other. I wanted to go, too, but I didn't dare to even ask Dad. I knew he would refuse. Instead, I helped Jadati cook and spent longer than usual on the swing that hung from the big olive tree. The peaceful rhythm of sailing up and down in the air calmed my nerves a bit.

We were gathered in the sitting room at lunch when Dad's phone rang. In those days, that nearly always meant bad news. He took the call, and we were all silent while he listened. His only words were "Oh God." He muttered that again and again. By the time he hung up, all the color had drained out of his face.

"What happened?" we all said in unison.

"Another massacre," he said slowly. Thousands of people had marched in the funeral procession. Security forces opened fire on them. They also shot at people who were on their way to the funeral procession. Some people who drove to the funeral were stopped by security agents who fired into the air. When they got out of the cars with their hands up to show that they presented no threat, security forces shot at them, too.

By that night, the bodies had been counted. Over two days, thirty-four people had been killed in Izraa alone. Among them were three boys younger than me and a grandfather in his seventies. The news shows said that the Izraa massacre was the largest massacre of the Syrian revolution.

That is, until larger massacres took that title away.

The pattern repeated.

Demonstrations would end in killings. Killings led to funerals. Funerals became new demonstrations. Week after week. In one town after another. All over Syria. Violence didn't scare people from protesting. It only brought more people to support the revolution.

Graffiti with anti-regime slogans used to be unimaginable. By May, it was all over town. At some point, the government made it illegal to buy spray paint.

On *The Opposite Opinion*, debates grew more intense. And that wasn't the only place where Syrians were at odds. The country was divided. Anyone in town could be an informant, reporting to the police about people who supported the revolution.

We were convinced that one of our neighbors, Um Safi, was an informant. She had a lot of connections to people in high places. She'd sneak around to figure out who was with the opposition and then report them. Um Safi was too sly to ask people about their views. Instead, she'd wait for someone to say something about politics accidentally. The word would hover there in the air and then she'd snatch it. She came over to my aunts' houses from time to time to have coffee and chat. My aunts were careful not to say anything around her.

Nayef's store became a dangerous place. Nayef was always talking about how the protesters were terrorists and the army would defeat our enemies. Military officers would come from the base to do their shopping at his store, and he'd greet them with excessive praise.

Then one intelligence officer began coming to the shop every other day. Then every day. Then he started spending the entire day in the shop. And then he actually moved in with Nayef and his wife!

Behind his back, we called him "Nayef's son." In front of him, we didn't say a thing. From behind the crates of onions and tomatoes, he spied on the whole neighborhood. He watched people while they bought groceries and listened to them as they made small talk. He learned everything about everyone. And his presence kept us silent.

Um Safi and Nayef's son were clear threats. Other threats were not so clear. In school, it was as if nothing was happening. Teachers never said a word. And I never talked to anyone at school about the revolution. It was safest not to trust anyone.

For Dad, the exception to that rule was his best friend, Abu Faysal. They weren't afraid to speak frankly with each other. One night Abu Faysal came over and I heard them arguing in the sitting room.

"These protests are wrong," Abu Faysal said. "The most important thing for our country is security and stability."

"The people want freedom," Dad said.

"They need to be patient. Now is not the right time."

"When will *ever* be the right time?" They were silent for a moment. Then Dad said, "Friend, I respect your opinion . . . even if it's wrong!"

They both burst out laughing. From where I sat in the kitchen, I smiled, too. And for a moment, I thought that things might turn out all right after all. Maybe our country could have freedom and security, too.

I never thought that so many years would pass without either.

PART III

UNDER THE BOMBS

October 2011

*Safety. It's strange how quickly something you
never thought about before can become the only
thing on your mind.*

Chapter 9

"*Takh takh takh takh*," Mohammed and Tayyim shouted as they pointed their sticks in our direction.

"*Takh takh takh takh*," Razi and I shouted back as we leaped from behind the bush where we'd been hiding. We sprinted between the trees. Mohammed and Tayyim ran after us, their "*Takh takh takh takh*" growing louder on our heels. I ran to one of my favorite trees, grabbed a branch, and threw myself on top of it, where no one could catch me. Below, Mohammed and Tayyim caught up with Razi and pointed their sticks directly at him. There was no escape. Razi dropped dramatically, crumpling like an empty bag of chips.

"Now *we* get to be the Free Army," Mohammed called up to me. "You guys got to be the Free Army three times this week. It's your turn to be the regime army."

War was now the focus of everything—even our games.

Huge peaceful demonstrations had continued into the summer. Deaths and arrests reached into the thousands. On news shows, call-in guests expressed frustration and despair.

"The world is standing by while they kill us. We need weapons to defend ourselves," one person demanded.

"The regime is trying to drag the opposition into a military battle. That is where the regime is strongest. The revolution should not fall into that trap," another warned.

"We never wanted an armed rebellion," another explained. "But we cannot endure this any longer."

The conflict on the streets made its way into the army, too. Most men in Syria were required to do military service. The army ordered soldiers to shoot at protesters. Many soldiers' hearts were on the side of the protests. Some started to escape from the army, though that was really dangerous to do. Eventually, some who defected declared that they were forming an alternative to the official Syrian Army. They called it the Free Syrian Army.

They became the new face of the revolution. Demonstrations became smaller and fewer. Instead, we heard about gun battles. In the city of Homs, Free Army brigades forced the regime to withdraw from large parts of the city. They declared neighborhoods to be liberated territory. Other towns and villages did the same.

Razi's older brother Mohammed joined the Free Army, too. He had studied computer science and was really good at all things related to computers. He helped the Free Army with media work.

"The revolution needs people who can fight in all sorts of ways, including with words," he told Razi.

For us younger ones, our fighting was imaginary and we

70

were always inventing new games that mirrored the conflict around us.

"I've got an idea!" Mohammed said. He was creative in that way. "Each team makes five guns and hides them," he explained. "Whichever team discovers the other team's arsenal wins."

I joined Tayyim and Razi to search the ground for fallen olive twigs that we could whittle into the shape of guns. I found two that could work. Then all of a sudden a real *takh takh takh* ripped through the air.

"Gunfire!" Razi said nervously.

"Get inside now!" we heard Dad yell from the house. The four of us raced inside, leaving our tree-branch guns behind.

We plopped down in the sitting room.

"I wish we could go play on the roof," Mohammed said.

In the early days of demonstrations, we had run to the roof excitedly whenever we heard the sounds of chanting in the distance. We had also run to the roof or out into the streets when we heard gunfire—we were that desperate to know what was happening. Dad was always yelling at us to get back inside. Then shooting from guns turned to shelling from the really big weapons stationed at the military base. There would be streams of heavy gunfire, like in war movies.

The military base that had been a normal part of our town suddenly felt like a monster hovering over us. Right now they were firing over our heads to other towns, where the Free Army was gaining strength. It was usually civilians who got killed, though.

The army wasn't bombing Izraa, because most people in Izraa had remained loyal to the regime. And as the base was so close, bombing our neighborhood would be like the army bombing itself.

When things were quiet, we'd go out and play. When they were not, we were stuck inside, as we were now. Streets became especially empty at night, when clashes between the Free Army and the regime usually happened. If Free Army fighters shot, the army fired all over the place with much more force. The next day, the army would raid houses in the area and search for weapons. Sometimes they'd burn motorbikes or arrest young men at random. They called it "combing."

Tayyim, Razi, Mohammed, and I watched TV and waited. When the shooting went silent, it seemed safe to go out again.

"I've got a new idea," Mohammed said. "Let's play house raid. The army comes, searches the house, and then sets it on fire."

Mohammed fetched one of Dad's cigarette lighters from the kitchen. The four of us headed outside again. We spread out in all directions to gather sticks and scraps of cardboard to build little houses. Then we set the roofs on fire and watched them collapse.

Chapter 10

Heaven, heaven, heaven! Our country is a heaven!...
Our country is beloved, even its fire is heaven!...
Revolt, Dara'a. Revolt! You are a candle in our
darkness!...

It was one of our favorite revolutionary songs, and Mohammed, Yousra, and I knew all the words.

"Heben, heben, heben, heben!" Zain sang along with us, shaking his hips to the beat. The rest of us tried to hold back our laughter.

"What's funny?" he asked, confused.

"Nothing," I said, pulling him onto my lap. "You're the best five-year-old singer in Syria."

I was alone watching my siblings while Dad was overseeing an exam at a school in Dara'a City. To get there, he had to cross many checkpoints where the army stopped people to look at their identity cards. They would check to see if you were on the lists of people wanted for arrest. The lists changed all the time, and you never knew if your name would be on one. Even if it wasn't, they could arrest you anyway. For any reason.

I'd turned on one of the new pro-revolution channels to distract us as we waited for Dad to return. The four of us spread out on the floor to watch.

"Even the thorns of my country are jasmine and roses, and its scent is heavenly," we sang.

The revolution had produced many new heroes. The singer of this song, Abdul Baset Al-Sarout, was one of those I loved most. He had been a goalie on the national soccer team, but he refused to play after the revolution began. He led huge demonstrations with his singing, inspiring people not to give up.

The sounds of cars on the street got in the way of the song. I peered out the window and saw a dozen cars and swarms of large, armed men.

"*Shabeeha*," I whispered. They were like a militia of huge men, with bulging muscles, foul mouths, and all sorts of weapons. I'd heard they beat people up, made arrests, and searched for evidence that someone was with the revolution. When they raided houses, they stole whatever they wanted or even worse. We called them beasts.

"What do they want?" Yousra asked fearfully.

"They must be doing house searches . . . ," I began. Before I could finish, we heard a knock at our door.

Shock waves went down my spine. Mohammed grabbed the remote control and clicked off the TV.

Be strong, I told myself. I was the oldest and responsible for my sister and brothers. I needed to be calm and brave so I could protect them. I went to the door and opened it.

"What do you want?" I asked, trying to stand tall.

"We're looking for terrorists and infiltrators," one said in a gruff voice.

"And searching for weapons," another barked.

"We have nothing to hide," I replied, my voice surprisingly steady. And then it hit me. We did have one thing to hide: Mohammed hadn't changed the channel before he turned off the TV. These men could turn on the TV if they wanted. And if they did, they'd see that we were watching a pro-revolution channel. That would be enough to make us guilty.

Stay calm, I told myself.

"Come in," I said, motioning.

Seven guys marched in. They walked through every room of the house. They opened closets, cabinets, and drawers.

Please don't check the TV, I thought, and silently recited the first verses of *surah Yasin* for protection.

They didn't. They finished and left. I went back to the sitting room and collapsed on a pile of pillows in relief. That relief didn't last long.

"Do you think they're going to Uncle Adnan's house? And to Aunt Fadiya's?" Yousra asked.

We all peered out the window carefully, so that no one could see us. *Shabeeha* were all over the streets, going to every house. Anything could happen.

We waited for hours. Eventually Dad made it home. And eventually we went over to Uncle Adnan's. The family told me that *shabeeha* came to their house, shouting and cursing. My cousin Aghiad knew that any young man was a potential target, because authorities suspected they were involved in the uprising in some way. So Aghiad opened the window, climbed out, and started running. They shot at him, but he managed to escape. He found his way to another relative's house, but he'd left a trail of blood behind him.

We feared it was no longer safe for Aunt Zihriya to stay in her apartment by herself, so she moved into the small house that my father had built in our backyard. Jadati sometimes stayed with us and sometimes with Aunt Zihriya.

House raids continued. When soldiers came to our neighborhood, Dad would tell us to keep playing so that they would see that everything was normal. But each time they came around, my siblings and I nervously rushed to the windows to see what was happening.

"You kids play all the time, except when you should keep playing. Then you just stop!" Dad would say.

Once when soldiers knocked on our door, Dad answered.

"Who is here in the house?" they demanded.

"I'm alone with my kids. Here's Muzoon, Mohammed, and Yousra." He pointed to each of us as we dropped our playing and gathered around him. "My son Zain is sleeping in the other room."

"Zain?" the soldiers asked suspiciously. "We want to see him."

Dad led them to the sitting room, where Zain was spread out on a mattress, napping. The soldiers turned on their heels in frustration. They were looking for rebel fighters but had found a kindergartner.

Another time, security force officers went to Aunt Fadiya's house. They looked around and found nothing. Then the commander pointed at Uncle Suleiman and my cousin Qutayba.

"You two, come with us," he ordered.

"But, sir, I'm a retired army colonel. My son hasn't—" Uncle Suleiman began to protest.

"Shut up," the commander interrupted. He pointed his gun, and the other officers grabbed them.

"Please, don't take them. Please, please," Aunt Fadiya cried. They ignored her as they marched her husband and son to the jeep. They got in and disappeared into the night.

Aunt Fadiya tried everything to get information. She called everyone she knew who might have power to help, who had connections to someone with power to help, or who had connections to someone who had connections to someone with power to help. She went to every police station in Izraa and then to police stations in the other towns and villages. But she wasn't able to learn anything.

We didn't know if Uncle Suleiman and Qutayba were alive or dead. Aunt Fadiya would come over in the evening to drink tea with Jadati, Aunt Zihriya, and Dad. Sometimes she would talk, but sometimes she would just sit, quietly. Razi stopped playing with us and would sit next to his mom instead. He was the baby of the family, and Aunt Fadiya had always been protective of him. Now she seemed to get nervous when he left her sight.

A month passed like that. A *month*. And then one day, without any warning, Uncle Suleiman and Qutayba came home. They were released with no explanation, just as they had been arrested with no explanation.

The whole family flocked to their house to welcome them back. They had lost a lot of weight. Their skin was pale, as if they hadn't seen sunlight since the day they disappeared. They took shower after shower but said they couldn't get rid of a feeling of filth. I guess it had gone more than skin deep.

We cousins went into the other room to play, but I tried to keep one ear on the adults' conversation. Some words rose to the top of the chatter like foam on the top of brewing Arabic coffee: "torture," "beating," "overcrowded," "humiliation," and "not even allow us to use the toilet."

There was only one thing I heard clearly. "Death is more merciful than prison," Uncle Suleiman said. "I will die before I ever go back there again."

Chapter 11

One Monday I arrived at school a bit early. I saw my friend Riham, and went over to say hi.

"How's it going?"

"Fine—how are you?"

"Good."

"Did you study for the math test?"

"Sort of. And you?"

"Sort of."

"Yeah."

"Yeah."

Our conversation floated, as light as air. In many ways our friendships continued as they always had. All of us girls had bought memory books at the beginning of the school year. After ninth grade we might head to different high schools. We wanted souvenirs to make sure we remembered each other. My book was thin and tan, with flowers on the cover and a real metal lock that closed with a miniature key. We passed our books around and wrote messages to each other filled with hearts, flowers, "friends forever," "I hope your dreams come true," and other sweet thoughts.

On the surface, school was normal. Below the surface, so much had changed. Everyone knew what was going on in the country, but no one dared to speak about it. I wouldn't say a word about politics because I couldn't trust anyone completely. And I suppose they didn't trust me.

The bell rang to begin morning assembly. I took a place in the eighth-grade B line. Looking around the courtyard, I noticed many new faces. Families were fleeing towns that the army was bombing. Many made their way to Izraa, rented apartments, and sent their kids to school. Everyone referred to them as tenants. Only much later did I understand that they were actually displaced people, or refugees.

We all stood as tall and stiff as we could to sing the national anthem:

Guardians of the homeland, upon you be peace.
Our proud spirits refuse to be humiliated....

In the past, I sang those words with pride. Now I felt confused. Who was guarding the homeland, and who was hurting it?

Assembly finished and everyone shuffled toward their classrooms. We went through the morning subjects: history, geography, biology, English. I was more motivated to study than I had ever been. I was so upset about the unfairness and cruelty around me that I wanted to do something about it, but didn't know how I could make a difference. I figured that the least I could do was work hard at school.

At noon, Arabic class began. Mr. Fares was conjugating subjunctive verbs on the board. I copied each word carefully in my notebook.

Mr. Fares wrote out different forms of "to listen." "The subjunctive mood is used to express a request, demand, or suggestion," he explained. "I suggest that you listen closely." He looked up at us, giving an example and a warning in one sentence. Mr. Fares was clever that way.

I listened closely. And beyond the squeak of Mr. Fares's black marker, I heard the faint echo of gunfire. Mr. Fares heard it, too, and paused. The shooting seemed far away. Mr. Fares's marker returned to the board.

"The subjunctive mood is also used for hypothetical situations," he continued. "For example, what if we were to—"

Suddenly the principal charged into the room.

"Everyone needs to go home immediately!" he shouted. Then, as quickly as he had appeared, he disappeared to pass the order on to the next classroom.

It is recommended that everyone leave, I said silently to myself in the subjunctive. *If I were you, I would get out of here.*

No one else seemed interested in the grammar of the situation. My classmates jumped to their feet and flew to the door without even zipping their backpacks. I snapped out of my thoughts, grabbed my stuff, and ran.

Hundreds of kids flooded down the stairs and into the

yard. I searched and searched for Mohammed, with no luck. There was a bottleneck at the gate as everyone tried to get out at the same time.

I felt some shoving behind me. "Hurry up—there's going to be an attack," someone said. "They're going to start bombing any minute," someone else cried out.

I began to panic. What attack? What bombing? Where? Was my family safe?

I made it out of the gate and walked fast in the direction of home. Surely Mohammed was heading home, too. What-ifs pounded in my head. What if the house was bombed? Jadati was there. What if Dad couldn't make it through the checkpoints on the way from work? What if there was fighting on the streets near Yousra and Zain's school? My mind was a jumble of hypotheticals, none conjugated correctly.

I walked as quickly as I could through the rocky shortcut, my heart keeping pace with my feet, fear fueling every step. What if my family were killed and I was left alone? I remembered a news story about a father whose apartment building was bombed while he was out looking for bread for his kids. "I wish I'd died with them," he moaned. He sat in the rubble, swearing that he would never leave them again.

I felt my lips quiver and my eyes well up, but I kept walking fast. At last I reached Nayef's store. Our house was at the top of the hill. I ran the last part of the way and was out of breath when I got to the door. I threw off my shoes and bolted in.

"Is anyone home?" I choked out through a stream of tears.

"What's wrong?" I heard Jadati's voice before I saw her

head poke out from the kitchen. "Are you hurt? Why are you home so early?"

She came toward me, wiping her hands on a dish towel.

"You're alive," I managed to say. "Is everyone else alive?"

She looked at me curiously.

"The attack . . . ," I began, unsure how to finish.

She must have read the rest on my face. "There's no attack," she said soothingly. "Everything is normal."

I collapsed onto Jadati in a way I hadn't since I was Yousra's age. Jadati held me tight. I heard a rumble of gunfire in the distance. It never came closer.

Everyone came home safely that day.

Chapter 12

Wissssssssssssssssss boom!

"Open the windows!" Dad shook me awake and ran out of the room.

I opened my eyes, disoriented. I wrestled off the thick winter blankets, stumbled sleepily to my feet, and unlatched the windows before Dad called out a second time.

Fall had become winter, and the war kept escalating. When there was bombing from the military base, the blasts could shatter windows in the surrounding neighborhood. We learned to stay as far from the windows as possible. We also learned to open them, which lessened the pressure, so they were less likely to break. The hard part was doing that on a cold February day.

"Get up." I nudged Yousra and then Zain as I gathered a mountain of blankets in my arms. The room where we slept was in the direct line of fire from the military base. The opposite corner of the house, in the room where we received guests, was safer. I hurried my siblings there. We joined Jadati, who was already huddling in the corner. Dad and Mohammed were going from room to room to make sure every window was open.

Wisssssssssssssssss boom!

"It's a missile launcher," Zain said.

"No, it's mortar shells," Yousra corrected him. "Missile launchers go *shuuuuuuuuuuu*. Mortar shells sound like *wissssssssssssssssss boom*."

Home had always been a safe place. The comfy pillows in the sitting room, the refreshing breeze on the roof, the smell of Jadati's cooking in the kitchen—home was where I could throw off my shoes, stretch out, and know that I was surrounded by family. I was lucky to be surrounded by family still. But I no longer felt safe. Anxiety and fear coated every surface of our home.

Dad and Mohammed finished their rounds and crouched with us under the blankets.

Buvvvv buvvvv buvvvv buvvvv buvvvv buvvvv!

We put our hands over our ears.

"That one was artillery," Zain said. Yousra nodded.

Even the littlest kids had become experts in the sounds of war. Sometimes the blasts from the army base were deafening. That meant that they were launching very powerful rockets aimed at a village far away. It could take a minute to hit the target, and we'd be looking as hard as we could to see where. If the bomb hit an empty field, it would not produce much smoke. If it hit a building or a vehicle, a gray mushroom cloud would puff into the air.

When the blasts were just normal loud, they were bombing

closer by. That was the kind of bombing that woke us up that night. Now our challenge was to distract ourselves from the fear and the cold pouring in through the windows. If I allowed myself to think, I would remember that we could be killed at any minute. The best hope to make it to sunrise was Jadati.

"Can you tell us a story?" I asked, huddling closer to her. When I was little, I'd ask Jadati to tell me a story every night before I went to sleep. Sometimes she told me about life when she was a girl—about how hard it was without electricity, running water, or schools. Other times she made up fantastic fairy tales about talking animals or imaginary kingdoms.

"A story at a time like this?" Jadati asked.

"Is there a better time?" I asked.

"Okay," she conceded, and began her tale.

Jadati's voice settled around us like a blanket.

Floodlights from nearby tanks circled the sky. The lights were so bright that when they flashed through the windows, they lit up the room as if it were the middle of the day. Every few minutes, a ball of fire flew through the darkness and the entire house shook.

The explosions kept us up the whole night. But as long as Jadati spoke, I felt safe.

Chapter 13

Eighth grade ended, summer vacation began, and the war continued. The reports of deaths and destruction stopped shocking me. We got used to it. *"Aadi,"* people would say. Normal. War had become normal.

Anyway, violence wasn't our only worry. It was harder and harder for people to work. Dad's school was bombed and completely destroyed. He was assigned to work at a different school, in an area that the army was also bombing hard. Parents didn't feel safe sending their kids to school, so no one came. His bosses told Dad to stop coming to work. I was glad he wasn't going into danger every day. But it also meant that he no longer got a salary.

At the same time, the prices of things kept rising. For as long as I could remember, a package of bread cost fifteen Syrian lira. Then it became nineteen lira. That might not seem like a lot, but for people already struggling, the difference was huge. Then bread was hardly available at all. With all the checkpoints and road closures, it was harder to get supplies like wheat and flour into the towns and cities. This was a disaster, because we Syrians eat bread with every meal.

Dad did whatever he could to find bread for us. He'd wake up before sunrise and stand in line at the bakery, hoping he might get some before they ran out. Once he and Mohammed roamed the whole city trying to find bread, without success. I stopped thinking about cookies or ice cream. Bread was everything.

Then the electricity started cutting out for hours or days. Some of the power plants had been destroyed by the bombing, so they'd cut the power to reduce the strain on the system. Sometimes it seemed like they cut power for no reason at all. Without TV, we had no idea what was happening around us. Without the refrigerator, food would spoil. We could no longer pay the water bill, so we cut back on water however possible. We used as little water as we could to wash dishes. We bathed infrequently. I'd wear the same clothes for months without washing them.

That year, Ramadan fell from mid-July to mid-August. During Ramadan, Muslims don't eat or drink anything from sunrise to sunset. When Mohammed and I were about seven and eight, we insisted on starting with mini-fasts until noon, even though we broke the fast if there was something really tasty around. By age ten, I was doing the full fast.

Ramadan had always been my favorite time of the year. It had a feel and spirit all its own. Relatives visited each other every evening after sundown. We'd cook fancy dishes and send some to Uncle Adnan or Aunt Fadiya. Their families would send part of what they cooked back to us. We also usually went to visit Aunt Fatima and her family. During the spring and summer, they moved to the countryside to herd goats and sheep. They'd live in a Bedouin tent, called a "hair house" because it was made of hair from their animals. There we'd cook over an open fire.

Ramadan now was different. Traditional treats, like little pancakes served with rosewater syrup or juice made from dried apricots, were out of the question. We couldn't travel to visit Aunt Fatima. Her son had gotten married, and he and his wife had a baby girl. We really wanted to see them, but it was just too dangerous.

Worst of all, the regime was using the holy month as another way to torment people. At sundown, mosques broadcast the call to prayer, signaling that it was time to break the fast. Precisely at that moment, we'd hear blasts from the military base. The army started to bomb families the second they sat to eat together.

Once that summer, on a day the electricity happened to be on, Dad was watching a program on Al Jazeera. It was a story about Syrians who had fled to Jordan. They were living in the middle of the desert in a place called Zaatari. The reporter was interviewing people about why they had left Syria. One woman explained that her village was being bombed. "Every night seemed like it could be our last," she said.

A man explained, "I couldn't work, so I couldn't feed my kids anymore. I needed to find them something better."

The reporters referred to these people as "Syrian refugees." I knew about Palestinian refugees and Iraqi refugees who had come and found safety in Syria. But I'd never thought about Syrians leaving to find safety somewhere else. I'd never heard the words "Syrian" and "refugee" spoken together. To my ears, that combination sounded like a mistake. Or like the screech of a musical instrument out of tune.

I felt sad for the people who left. Yes, there was war, but we needed to be strong. I thought it was wrong for people to abandon their land and homes.

"These people should come back to Syria," I said as I marched out of the room. I didn't want to hear any more about it.

Fall came and I began ninth grade. This was the most important academic year of my life. At the end of ninth grade, you took a national exam that determined what you would study in high school. High school, in turn, affected whether you would go to college.

My dream of going to college motivated me to study hard. All the bad news did, too. One of the worst things about this war was that it made you feel helpless. Learning made me feel capable and strong. School was the one place where things kept moving in a positive direction.

But it wasn't easy. As the bombing got worse, sometimes school was canceled or it became too dangerous to get there. With no electricity, I did all the studying I could during daylight hours and then read by candlelight at night. Sometimes we worried that rockets or missiles could hit the house, and we found shelter outside instead. We had a fig tree that grew in the center of a huge round ditch. We stood in that deep hollow, with the tree above our heads like a canopy. Depending on the bombing, we might stay for fifteen minutes or for hours. I'd bring my books with me and study until it was safe to go inside again.

Fall moved toward winter, and the trees lost their leaves. The cold set in, but gas for the space heater became too expensive. Some of my best memories were of sitting around the heater. The whole family would circle around it, sharing the warmth. Sometimes I fell asleep there, even though Jadati always warned me that was dangerous. When we were little, Mohammed and I used to put bread directly on the heater to warm it. Dad would get angry, because the bread would stick.

But no gas meant no heater. We started using charcoal instead, and then wood. One of our neighbors would stay warm by burning nylon and other fabrics. I would hold my nose, but I couldn't block out the suffocating smell. It gave me migraines.

The news that we managed to hear was all bad.

New Year's Eve came, but no one was in a mood to ring in 2013 with cheer. It was hard to believe that only two years had passed since Aunt Zihriya and I celebrated with chocolate cake with sparkle frosting, and I'd swiped the bowl clean with my fingers. I was such a kid back then. I could hardly recognize myself.

PART IV

THE MOST
IMPORTANT THINGS

January 2013

What is most important? Your home? Your family?
Your country? Your school? Your life? Most people
don't have to choose. But we did.

Chapter 14

I remember the first time I heard them mention it. It was an unusually warm winter day. Tayyim and Mohammed were playing in the yard. I was pacing back and forth as I studied biology. Uncle Adnan, Aunt Ayida, and Dad sat under an olive tree. I caught bits of their conversation each time I walked by them.

"We need to consider it," Uncle Adnan said.

The seriousness of his tone caught my attention.

"How can we be sure it's safe?" Dad asked.

"Well, we know it's no longer safe here," Uncle Adnan replied.

What were they talking about? The more I heard, the more difficult it was to focus on the difference between pro-karyotic and eukaryotic cells. Their conversation continued.

"There's a camp in Jordan for Syrian refugees," Aunt Ayida said.

There it was again: *Syrian refugees.* My heart started beating faster. This was not good.

"It's called Zaatari," she said.

It was the same name that I'd heard mentioned on TV.

"But we don't know anything about the camp."

"It might offer us a better life."

"It might."

"Are there schools there?"

I froze as my heart began to thump in my chest. The pictures of nuclei, ribosomes, and mitochondria blurred into blobs as I waited for Uncle Adnan's response to Dad's question.

"Maybe. I hope so. *Inshallah.*"

Maybe? God willing? I slammed my biology book shut.

"Are you talking about leaving Syria?" I demanded. I was surprised to hear my voice shake with anger.

Uncle Adnan and Dad turned to me, no less surprised.

"Muzoon . . . ," Dad began, struggling to find a voice that would calm me.

I continued, "If we leave Syria, will that be the end of my education?"

Dad put his hand on his heart. "You know that your education means the world to me," he said.

I did not budge. "If we leave Syria, will that be the end of my education?" I asked again.

"I don't know," Dad said. "But schools are not sure here, either. Nothing is certain in Syria."

The discussion continued for about a month. Sometimes Uncle Adnan's family would come to our house. Sometimes we'd go over there. When it was warmer, Uncle Adnan and Dad would talk outside under the trees. When the temperature dropped, the conversation continued under blankets inside. One day they'd decide we should stay, and I'd be relieved. The next day they'd agree we should go, and I'd become upset all over again.

It turned out that Abu Majed, one of Dad's distant cousins, had left for Zaatari in Jordan a few months ago. Uncle Adnan made contact with him to ask what it was like. Abu Majed couldn't talk long, but his message came through. "Life here is hard," he said. "But life in the camp is better than death in Syria."

Dad told Jadati that we were thinking of leaving. She said that he should do what was best for us kids. "But I'm too old to go anywhere," she added. "I will die in my own country before I live as a stranger in a foreign land." For Jadati, that was the beginning and the end of the story. There was no negotiating with her when she'd made up her mind. And as long as Jadati stayed, Aunt Zihriya would stay with her. Aunt Fadiya and Aunt Fatima and their families also had no plans to leave.

But my family and Uncle Adnan's family endlessly weighed pros and cons. No one *wanted* to go, but most of them felt that it was the smart thing to do.

Except for me.

I rejected it completely and defended that point of view in every conversation.

Tayyim and I talked about it one day as we took turns on the swing.

"I think we should go," he said, kicking his legs and soaring upward.

"That's easy for you to say. You're in eighth grade—there's not much to lose."

"I guess," he said as he floated back down.

"My life depends on ninth grade. If we leave, my future might be over."

"None of us will have futures if we get killed."

"How do you know we will get killed?" I insisted.

Later, I talked about it with Dad and Mohammed as we cleared the lunch plates.

"I just want you kids to have a better life," Dad tried to persuade me.

"How do you know that Zaatari will be better than here?" I snapped. "Did you go there? Can you prove it?"

"Only God knows," Dad replied. "But there is war here, and there is no war there."

Mohammed nodded, and I felt betrayed. Why did no one see this my way?

I knew that Uncle Adnan and Dad were more concerned about us kids than they were about themselves. That was the case for a great many Syrian parents. Uncle Adnan was worried because his two oldest sons were near the age of mandatory military service. Soon they would have to go into the army, where they would kill or die or both. Dad was worried because he was our only parent at home. If something happened to him, what would become of the four of us? For him, every time he left the house felt like a terrifying risk.

Being at home was terrifying, too. One night, our neighborhood filled with jeeps as soldiers searched street by street. They entered people's homes and came out leading men they had arrested.

I poured myself into my books, trying not to think about if and when they would knock on our door.

The next day was especially cold. Uncle Adnan had searched all over town and managed to find gas for the heater, so we all gathered around it at his house. As ever, the adults talked about leaving.

"We can't go on like this."

"Maybe the situation will get better?"

"It's been almost two years, and things have only gone from bad to worse."

"The revolution . . ."

"Human life has become cheaper than bread."

"This is the hardest decision of my life. I feel like I'll be leaving part of myself."

"I know. Let's just give it a try. We can go for ten days and then come back."

"Just ten days?"

"Just ten days."

"Okay. Ten days. We'll try."

Chapter 15

Dad and Uncle Adnan started making practical arrangements. I continued to study as normal. I did my homework and went to class each day. At school I didn't speak a word to anyone. The government viewed those who fled the country as traitors abandoning the homeland. Talking about leaving would only put us at risk.

Besides, I still held out hope that Dad and Uncle Adnan might reconsider. Or maybe the situation in Syria would change. Maybe other countries would get involved and stop the war. Anything could happen. All I knew was that I needed to keep studying. It was the one thing I could control. Life felt like a raging storm at sea. School was my life preserver, and I was going to hold on to it as long as I could.

One Tuesday afternoon Dad came into the sitting room, where I was preparing for a geography exam while my siblings watched cartoons.

"Tomorrow . . . ," he said.

I had little doubt about what was coming but still hoped his pause would last forever.

". . . we leave."

It felt like a punch to the stomach.

"Everyone pack a bag," he continued. "Just take your most important things."

There was nothing left for me to say. Zain was too little to grasp what was happening to us. Yousra and Mohammed got out their school backpacks. They emptied them and started rummaging through their closets.

I followed Dad as he went to the living room and opened the chest of drawers. That was where he kept all our important documents. He took papers out one by one and examined each: our birth certificates, his college teaching diploma, his training certificates from various teaching workshops, and so on. He placed them all in a stiff brown envelope.

"What are you doing?" I asked.

"It's too risky to take these documents with us. We don't know what might happen on the journey. I need to leave them with someone we can trust to keep them safe."

It was starting to feel real. I turned and went back to where Mohammed and Yousra were packing.

Just take your most important things, I said to myself, turning over Dad's words in my mind.

Yousra held up her backpack proudly.

"Finished!" she said, beaming.

"What are you bringing?" I asked.

Yousra peeked inside her backpack and named each item

like she was reading a grocery list. "My teddy bear, three shirts, two pairs of pants, three pairs of socks, my Sponge Bob diary, two pencils, and the hair bow that Aunt Zihriya gave me last Eid."

Mohammed zipped his backpack and tossed it by the door. "What did you pack?" I asked.

He shrugged. "A change of clothes."

"That's it?"

"We're only going for ten days." He shrugged again.

From the closet I took out the duffel bag that I used to pack clothes when I spent summers at Aunt Zihriya's apartment.

Your most important things, I thought again.

I put each of my nine schoolbooks inside, one after the other: history, math, geography, Arabic grammar, Arabic literature, English, biology, chemistry, and physics. I put my memory book on top and zipped the bag shut.

That evening there was a knock at the door. Dad had invited Abu Faysal over for coffee. They sat together under one of our trees for their usual small talk. The soft hum of their voices helped me to study. Yes, even that night I was studying!

After an hour or so, I sensed a shift in the conversation. It was suddenly quiet. I looked up and saw that Dad had handed a brown envelope to his friend.

"What is this?" Abu Faysal asked.

"It's our important documents. Please keep them safe," Dad said.

They were quiet for several moments. Dad did not tell

Abu Faysal that we were leaving Syria. Abu Faysal did not ask. But they both understood. They knew it might be their last goodbye.

Abu Faysal held the envelope to his heart and said simply, *"Amanah."*

Amanah means a moral obligation to fulfill the trust that someone puts in you. It is a very special word in our society. Jadati taught me that it was originally an Islamic concept, meaning a duty to God. But all Arabs use it, Muslim or not. We'd actually studied the word in Arabic class. Mr. Fares pointed out that *amanah* stems from the root meaning safety and security. You make something secure when you give it to a person of trust. And in making it secure, that person makes you feel secure, too.

I don't think there was much that could make Dad feel secure that sad day. We were heading into the unknown, and Dad was as worried as I was. But the promise of a true friend must have helped a little.

Many years have passed, and Abu Faysal is still holding that envelope for us. *Amanah.*

I didn't sleep at all that night. Questions exploded in my head like popcorn. Would this be my last night in my house? What would life be like in a refugee camp? Would the whole family ever be together again? How would I continue my education if there were no schools? I listened to my sleeping siblings' deep breaths and muffled my crying so I would not wake them.

Uncle Adnan had arranged for a minivan to pick us up. Before it arrived, Dad and I walked over to the small house to say goodbye to Jadati. Dad bent down and kissed her hand, as children do to their parents as a sign of love and respect. I gave her a long and tight hug. No words could say more than that hug.

It was a normal workday, and Aunt Zihriya was at her school. During her break she drove home and met us near Nayef's shop.

"It's not too late to reconsider," she said, trying to persuade Dad one last time. When he shook his head, she said something that surprised me. "Leave Muzoon with us. She can finish ninth grade. We'll figure out what to do after that."

"I can't leave a young girl here by herself." Dad looked pained. "If anything happened to her . . ."

Aunt Zihriya looked to me. "What do you think, Muzoon?"

I loved her for asking. For trying to give me a choice. But I knew that I couldn't put that burden on my father. And I knew I couldn't stay here without my family. They were my most important things.

So for the first time, I said, "I want to go."

Still, I couldn't stop myself from crying as I hugged Aunt Zihriya goodbye.

"Don't worry, my love," Aunt Zihriya said as she squeezed me tight. "We'll make *harissa* when you're back. We'll get everything just right."

Chapter 16

Dad and Uncle Adnan got into the front seat of the mini-van with the driver. Aunt Ayida, my three siblings, my seven cousins, and I all piled into the back.

I folded my arms flat along the car windowsill and rested my chin on my hands. I silently said goodbye to everything. To the grapevines that canopied the front door of our house. To the trees that I'd climbed or picked or that had kept me company while I studied. To the stone walls that had been our soccer boundaries. To streets where I'd learned to ride a bike. To the buildings and shops and other houses that had been the markers on my walks. To the elementary school where I'd met the kids who had been my classmates every single year since kindergarten. To the air, the rocks, the grass, the gravel. To people on the street who I didn't know, but who were a part of my hometown.

I wanted to look in every direction at the same time. I wanted to hold it all in my sight as long as I could. I was leaving behind everything I'd ever known. It felt like the end of the world to me.

The farther we got, the sadder I felt. I cried and didn't even try to stop myself from crying in front of the others. Aunt Ayida and Yousra cried, too. Uncle Adnan and Dad didn't cry. Nor did my older cousins. But you could see in their eyes that they were miserable. The little kids, like Zain and my younger cousins, didn't understand what was happening. They jumped around the back of the van, having fun with the large open space. Emirate, my cousin who was still an infant, slept in Aunt Ayida's arms.

We came to the edge of Izraa and held our breath as we passed through a regime checkpoint. For this I dried my eyes and tried to act like everything was normal. If the soldiers suspected that we were leaving the country, they could arrest us or take my cousins away for military service. But they just waved us through.

To avoid more checkpoints, the driver took back roads through areas that were under control of the Free Army. These were the places that the military base had been bombing all those months.

The destruction was beyond anything I'd imagined. Most buildings had their front walls torn off. It was like they were cakes sliced in half, exposing inside layers. Some buildings had collapsed completely and were just piles of rubble. Many cars were scorched.

Syrian streets are usually full of life, but these streets were empty. *Where are all the people?* I asked myself. *What happened to all the kids who should be out playing?*

I realized that I had experienced the war mostly through sounds. In Izraa, we were used to hearing rockets or missiles whiz over our heads. Now I was catching a glimpse of what happened when those missiles actually exploded, and something in me shifted. I understood why people were becoming refugees. They were fleeing for their lives.

We arrived at a city called Taybeh. It was the last Syrian town before the border with Jordan. We piled out of the minivan. Free Army fighters led us to a basement in a community center. It was filled with people who were leaving, just like us.

"Women and children on one side, men on the other," a fighter directed us.

It was so crowded and noisy. I didn't want to get stuffed in with all these people. My face got warm and my pulse raced. I was on the edge of panic.

"I want to go home," I said, grabbing Dad's arm before he descended to the men's section.

"Muzoon, be patient," he responded.

"Is this what the refugee camp will be like?"

"No, God willing. I don't think so," he said. "Here we wait until sundown. Then we'll complete the journey."

I followed Aunt Ayida to the women's section and sat on the floor. I regretted having ever agreed to come. Every so often I muttered under my breath, "I want to go home" or "We should never have left." I just couldn't stop myself.

Slowly, my anger wore itself out and turned into boredom. I needed to move.

"Hey." I waved to Mohammed and Tayyim, who were

over in the men's section. I caught their attention and used hand gestures to tell them that we should go out and look around.

"And ask Dad for money," I mouthed. They gave me a thumbs-up.

A few minutes later, the three of us were out on the street, buying candy from a guy selling snacks there. Then we went to investigate the empty rooms of an abandoned house nearby.

"I bet the regime will fall before we cross the border," Mohammed said, bouncing on the couch in what had once been some family's living room.

"Then we can just turn around and go home!" Tayyim added.

Eventually our parents called us back to the basement. We returned to waiting.

Hours passed and the sky dimmed with evening light. Four trucks appeared. One of the fighters shouted to the group, "Women in these two, men in the others. Squeeze in as close as you can."

Squeeze, indeed. The back of the truck was open to the sky. When I stepped in, there were already more women than I could count. After us, more and more women crammed in. I stood sandwiched between a dozen different bodies. I felt one body's elbow and another body's leg. Most of the women were older than me. I was a twig of a girl lost among their curves.

One young woman was probably in her early twenties. She kept looking at one of the fighters and blushing. "He's so handsome. Do you think he's married?" she asked another woman. Though I could hardly breathe, I somehow managed to burst into giggles. What a time to flirt!

Then the tailgate shut and the truck took off.

By the time we stopped, it was pitch-dark. Aunt Ayida, baby Emirate, Yousra, and I tumbled out of the truck and reunited with the male members of our family. The fighters made an announcement to the group.

"Everyone carry your things. We will walk to Jordan from here. It's about three hours. We are close to regime-controlled areas. If the army notices you, they'll shoot. You cannot shine any lights or make any noise. Your life depends on it."

I looked nervously around me.

"One more thing," the fighter added. "We need to walk quickly, but the path is filled with rocks. So don't trip."

The group started walking. Dad instructed the four of us to walk in front of him so he could keep an eye on us at all times. I grabbed my duffel bag and moved into the lead.

We walked and walked. And then kept walking. My mind emptied of any thought besides my next step. Walking in front of my family, I wanted to be strong and responsible. But my bag was so heavy. I shifted it from my right hand to my left and then from my left to my right. Each option made me lopsided in a different way.

"Muzoon," Dad whispered, "are you okay?"

I waved my hand as if to brush him off. I kept walking.

"Let me carry your bag," he whispered again.

"I can handle it," I replied automatically. But I didn't even convince myself. I tried carrying the bag with both hands at once, but that didn't work at all.

"Yes, can you help me?" I finally said softly, nervous to admit that I needed help.

I felt Dad's smile through the darkness as he reached out and took my bag.

"Good Lord, what did you bring? Your bag is heavier than the rest of our bags combined!"

"My schoolbooks," I mumbled.

"Your *what*?"

"My schoolbooks," I said again, too loudly.

"Keep quiet and keep moving!" another voice hissed in the dark.

"This must weigh twenty pounds. Why did you bring all this?" Dad asked, his voice filled with disbelief.

"You said to bring my most important things," I replied, defiant.

I could tell Dad was upset. But after a while he laughed quietly.

And on and on and on we walked.

Chapter 17

Around midnight we found ourselves walking down a hill. Jordanian Border Patrol officers ushered our group into a large tent. They gave us water and crackers that tasted like salty cardboard. I took one bite and gave the rest to Mohammed, but he didn't like it, either.

"Welcome to Jordan," he chuckled.

I didn't know which of the many steps we'd taken was the last in Syria. But for the first time in my life, I was no longer there.

The officers lined us up to register our names. Dad handed one of them our family book, which was the official Syrian document listing all members of a family. I watched as the officer wrote each of our names.

M-E-Z-O-O-N.

"You spelled my name wrong," I pointed out. My name is a special word for rain clouds. It's a very rare name. Dad had picked it out for his first daughter even before he got married.

The officer gave me a sharp look. He wasn't pleased that a

fourteen-year-old was correcting his Arabic. He looked away and called out, "Next!"

We piled into another truck, which took us to a place where we waited for a bus. The bus took us to a town called Mafraq, where the Zaatari camp was located.

After an hour, our bus stopped, but we still weren't at the camp. First we had to do some formal registration at an office in the center of town. The driver got out and told us to wait. And so we waited. And waited. And waited.

A full hour passed. "I need to go to the bathroom," Zain whined.

"Me too," Yousra chimed in.

But there was no getting off the bus. We waited. And waited. And waited. I kept the time by counting the number of kids who voiced their complaints.

"I'm thirsty." That made nine.

"I'm bored." Ten.

"It's so stuffy in here." Eleven.

"I can't breathe." Twelve.

"When are they going to let us out?" Thirteen.

Then the string of high-pitched kid complaints was broken by the deep voice of an old man sitting behind us. "I wish God had never created the road that brought us to this horrible place!" There were hours of pent-up frustration in that curse, but somehow it made me laugh. I put my hand to my mouth to stifle it.

After three hours, we descended from the bus and went into the office. We waited more. When it was our turn, Dad submitted his Syrian ID and the family book. The officer took them, filled out many forms, and waved us onward.

"Excuse me, sir—my documents?" Dad asked.

"They stay with us," the officer responded. "Next!"

We boarded another bus, which took us to Zaatari.

The camp was surrounded by a towering chain fence about twice as high as a tall man. In some places the fence was held up with thick metal stakes, in other places by long metal rods bent like drinking straws. Even an experienced tree climber was not going to be able to climb a fence like that. As I got closer, I saw that the top of the fence was barbed wire.

Darkness stretched in every direction, except for where overhead lights baked the area beneath in a strange golden glow. It felt like being under a giant flashlight. I would later learn that lights surrounded only the camp's front offices. The rest of the camp, where people lived, was sheer darkness.

"Keep walking to the reception hall, please," a voice called out.

We followed others into the largest tent I'd ever seen. Metal rods poked the cloth roof into a triangle.

"It looks like those circus tents in the cartoons," Zain said.

"Perfect for a clown like you," I teased him, trying to lighten the mood. It didn't work. We were too exhausted and too scared to laugh.

We entered through a big opening. A few gas space heaters warmed the air a bit, but the floor was cold dirt. Aid workers wearing special vests distributed blankets, mats, water, and more of those terrible crackers.

"Is this the only food in Zaatari?" I asked.

So many families crowded into the tent. Everyone was talking, and the place buzzed with noise.

I felt the same creeping panic I had in the basement where we'd waited to go to the border. But other feelings crowded in as well: Sadness about leaving Syria. Fear that we might get stuck here forever. Anger that we were herded around like sheep. Annoyance with the lack of privacy and quiet. Dizziness with how twenty-four hours had turned my life upside down.

It felt like our journey had lasted a month rather than a day. It barely even felt real. Like it was all a dream. Or a nightmare.

I was trying to focus my thoughts, but all the feelings got in the way. Exhaustion did, too.

"Muzoon, let yourself fall asleep," Dad urged in a gentle voice, recognizing the tension in my shoulders that pulled up to my ears as I clutched my bag of books.

"I cannot sleep with all this noise. In front of all these people," I said.

"I understand," he said with a heavy voice as he looked around the tent. "This is not what I expected, either."

"Is this what it's always going to be like?" I asked. "Sharing a tent with so many strangers?"

"I don't know."

"We need to go back home," I insisted. "We can't live like this."

"I'll look into it tomorrow." Dad nodded. "Now try to get some sleep."

I laid my head down on my bag of books, using it as a hard and lumpy pillow. I pulled my coat over my head. I held my hands over my ears in a useless attempt to block out the chatter. *It will be just ten days,* I told myself. *Just ten days.*

PART V

REFUGEES

February 2013

And now we began our lives as that thing that sounded so wrong to my ears: Syrian refugees. We were the same, but everything around us was strange and uncomfortable and unknown.

Newness is exhausting

Chapter 18

Morning announced itself when one of the babies in the tent began to cry. Baby Emirate joined in for a chorus of crying. This gradually woke up everyone around me—but I hadn't slept all night.

Dad's cousin Abu Majed came to the reception hall. Seeing family in a place like this gave me more comfort than I would have guessed.

"Welcome, welcome. We've been waiting for you," he said with a hearty laugh. There was an assembly line of hugs, handshakes, and a trio of pecks on the cheeks as he greeted all fourteen of us.

"Seham is preparing breakfast for you. Let's head home," he said, ruffling Zain's hair.

I could not imagine how anyone could be so cheerful in a place like this, or call it home. He must have seen the worry on my face. "It will get better," he told me. "Be patient."

We gathered our things and exited the tent, one after another. When my head poked outside, I nearly dropped my bag of books. A jolt of light struck, so bright that I covered my face and squeezed my eyes shut.

Slowly, I opened my eyes again. The light was actually a blinding whiteness. The camp was white, white, white. Everything was white. The ground was a kind of white pebble pressed into white sand. The white sand puffed into clouds of white dust. And fixed in the white ground were white tents. Rows upon rows of white tents.

The strong desert sunlight made the white even more intense. It was hard to see where the ground stopped and the tents started. There was just white and the blue of a cloudless sky.

In Syria, I was always surrounded by the green of trees. We'd gone from a lush paradise to a vast and empty desert. It was like being on the moon.

We kids spent most of the day with Abu Majed's wife, Seham, while Dad and Uncle Adnan went to the camp's administrative offices. Before Dad left, I pulled him aside.

"Please ask about how we return to Syria," I told him. "Please also find out about the school here." I realized that these two things were contradictory. But I needed to know that one option or the other was open to me. My entire future depended on it.

Dad nodded and then disappeared with Uncle Adnan into a cloud of white dust. When they reappeared several hours later, they were dragging tents and supplies, as well as registration cards for each of us.

The camp authorities had given Uncle Adnan two tents for his large family. Our smaller family was given one.

"We can set up our tent wherever we like," Dad said. He had explored the grounds and found an empty spot between two of the shared kitchen shelters. From then on, we would refer to our address as "between the two kitchens." It became our little patch of home in this world of white.

"Hold steady!" Dad called out as he set up our tent. Three of my older cousins each held down one corner of the tent. Mohammed and Tayyim worked as a team, pressing their full thirteen-year-old weight to pull the fourth corner to the ground.

After a lot of tugging and even some swearing, the tent was upright. We walked inside. Yousra and I echoed the same reaction.

"Is this it?"

"All five of us are going to live here?"

"It's a fraction of a fraction of the size of a room in our house in Syria!"

I couldn't imagine how we would sleep, eat, study, store our stuff, receive visitors, and live our lives in this cramped space. Dad tried to ease our sense of disappointment. "You are all strong, and we'll make it work," he said.

We began arranging the materials that the camp had given us, as they did all new families. We laid the mats on top of the thin layer of nylon that formed the bottom of the tent. In one corner we stored a cooking pot, a bucket, plastic jugs for water, metal dishes, and silverware. We folded the five blankets and stacked the five thin sponge mattresses.

These would serve as beds at night and something to sit on during the day.

"Where are the pillows?" Yousra asked.

"They didn't give us any," Dad said.

"How am I supposed to sleep without a pillow?" Zain demanded.

Mohammed looked at me and I looked at Dad and he looked down at the mattresses.

"I'll find a knife and cut one of the mattresses into pillows," he suggested.

Somehow, he managed to do that before we headed to bed that night.

"Now everyone has a pillow," he said, distributing the five slices. "When we sleep, we'll just have to squeeze together on four mattresses."

As we squeezed in, the questions began.

Mohammed wondered how we could manage without electricity. How would we find out what was happening in Syria without television?

Yousra wanted to know how soon we could leave.

Zain snuggled against Dad, not quite old enough to know what to ask.

Finally I asked the question that had been on my mind all day.

"Did you find out if there's a school?"

"All day, I asked everyone I met," he assured me.

"And?"

"There is one school in session, but it's on the far side of the camp. The term is ending soon."

My heart fell.

"But in April a new school is opening close to here."

"What does that mean?"

"In a month or so, you can go back to ninth grade."

A smile took over my face. I felt relief for the first time in days. Not total relief, but enough so that I was able to sleep that night. As I drifted off, I remembered Jadati's stories about her nomadic life as a girl. Now I, too, would reside in a tent. I, too, would live without electricity or running water.

But in one important way, my situation would be much better. As Jadati always reminded us, she never had the chance to go to school. I would.

Chapter 19

That night was the coldest I'd ever experienced.

"I thought deserts were hot," Zain said as we wrestled out of bed in the morning. Dry desert nights, we discovered, can be bone-chillingly cold. We also discovered how thin our tent and blankets were. From then on, we bundled as close as we could so that our layers of blankets could overlap.

My days of sleeping late were over, too. From now on, our lives would follow the rhythm of the sun. With no streetlights or electricity, it was impossible to see anything at night, so we'd go to bed shortly after dark. Then we'd wake up at dawn, as the bright sunlight made it impossible to keep sleeping.

Abu Majed came to our spot between the two kitchens to show us around the camp. As we walked along the gravel roads, I saw that Zaatari wasn't as white as my first impression. Most tents were covered by thick brown dirt and gritty dust. It wouldn't be long before our tent became brown, too.

Tents were also stamped with huge blue letters: "UNHCR," which I discovered stood for the United Nations High Commissioner for Refugees. That was the United Nations agency responsible for all refugee matters, including the camp.

"What are those?" Dad asked, pointing to a metal box like a trailer or camper.

"Caravans," Abu Majed explained. "They're much better to live in than tents. UNHCR is gradually trying to switch from tents to caravans. But meanwhile you can try to buy one from another family if you've got the money."

I thought about the savings that Dad had brought with him. But I doubted we had enough to buy one of those.

We followed Abu Majed and arrived at a street bustling with activity.

"Welcome to our commercial strip," Abu Majed laughed. "We call it the Champs-Élysées, like the luxury avenue in Paris."

My eyes widened as I took in the biggest souk I'd ever seen. The dusty path was filled with makeshift stalls built of any sort of scrap materials people could find. Stores sold cell phones, clothing, electronics, and furniture. There were beauty salons, bridal gown shops, cafés, kabob restaurants, and bakeries selling desserts like Aunt Zihriya and I tried to make. The sellers in their stalls called for people to come buy their vegetables, their coffee, their falafel. And everyone was talking about home, about the news, about what was going on in Syria.

"When did the camp set this up?" Dad asked.

Abu Majed gave out another laugh. "Residents did it for themselves, using the same business smarts they've always used. It started with just a few stalls. Now even Jordanians from outside the camp come here to buy from us."

The market sold everything you could imagine. The problem was that you needed money. I thought again about our savings. Dad must have thought about it, too. He took a few bills out of his pocket and turned to Abu Majed.

"Where can we buy some thicker blankets?" he asked.

During the days that followed, we each took on new responsibilities—the things we needed to do to survive in this place. Dad immediately started asking if there were opportunities for work as a teacher. Mohammed was in charge of bread and water. He'd wake up every morning and wait in line to get a fresh package of bread for the day. Next he'd take the bucket and the plastic jug and walk to one of the big water tanks. He'd carry the heavy load back to the tent, waddling like a duck. If the line for water was very long, he might walk on to another location. The water was yellowish and tasted funny. At first we used it only for cleaning and spent our precious savings to buy bottled water to drink. When we ran out of money, we started drinking the water that came from the faucets, like everyone else.

Either Dad or Mohammed would pick up the food basket. Every two weeks we got a box of dry goods: rice, bulgur, pasta, lentils, sugar, and salt. We also got some cans of green beans, hummus, tomato paste, and halva, which is a crumbly sweet made of sugar and sesame paste. I tasted the halva once and refused to go near it again. It was nothing like the halva we used to eat in Syria.

I was responsible for laundry, washing dishes, and other cleaning. As the oldest, I also took care of my siblings. Zain and Yousra were too little to have big jobs, but they helped to keep the tent swept and neat.

The biggest of my new duties was cooking for my family. I loved making desserts with my aunt. This was different.

First I had to decide what to make. I looked at our basket of food items that never changed. Should I make lentils and rice? Or lentils and bulgur? Or plain rice or plain bulgur? Or plain pasta? I hated pasta. On this particular day I decided to make lentils and rice.

Then I put everything I needed into the pot, so I could carry it to the kitchen. The kitchens were concrete shelters with a wall in the middle. On either side of the wall was a row of six stovetop burners.

The next step was tricky: figuring out which kitchen to go to, and at precisely what time, so that it wouldn't be too busy. With so many people in the camp, the kitchens were almost always busy. Sometimes you had to wait a long time for a burner.

The hardest part for me at first was doing all this with an audience. There were nosy ladies who stretched their necks to look into your pot and comment on your cooking, even though everyone had identical pots and was making some variation of the same thing. Others would ask all sorts of prying questions that had nothing to do with cooking. The kitchens were filled with chatter as much as with the aromas of cooking rice, bulgur, and pasta.

Camp kitchens became so famous for gossip that Zaatari residents called rumors "kitchen news." When a piece of information began to circulate, we'd ask, "Is that real news or kitchen news?"

Eventually I'd spot an available burner and put my pot there.

The next step in cooking was to guess at exactly the right amount to get the five of us through the day. We had no refrigerator, so there was no way to store leftovers without them going bad or attracting a swarm of ants. I made my guess and poured the rice and water into the pot. No sooner had I done that when the questions began.

"You must be new here! What's your name? Where are you from?" one of the ladies asked. She wore a long black abaya, a robelike dress that stretched to the ankles.

"My name is Muzoon. I'm from Izraa," I replied. Nearly everyone in Zaatari was from Dara'a Province. The question of where you were from usually required only the name of your town.

"What are you cooking?"

"Rice and lentils."

"Hmm—I cooked that yesterday."

"You don't know how lucky you are to be cooking at all!" another woman said, her bracelets jangling as she stirred her pot. "We arrived right after the camp opened. There were no kitchens then. A truck would come in and distribute boxes of pre-prepared meals."

"Don't remind me," another lady added. She fixed her bright blue headscarf and turned her burner to a low flame. "Those meals were inedible. Once, I got a piece of chicken that still had feathers on it."

Everyone laughed. I giggled, too.

"Once they realized we were going to be here for a while, they made these kitchens," the lady in bright blue continued. "And now we get to cook the same rice and pasta every day!"

The lady with the bracelets held up a small bottle and let a few drops fall into her pot. "This is my secret ingredient," she said. She kept stirring, and her rice turned a deep golden yellow.

"We might not have spices," she said, shrugging. "But food coloring tricks my kids into thinking the rice has flavor!"

We all laughed again. Maybe the kitchens weren't so bad, I thought. Then the lady in the abaya turned to me and asked another question. It was that old question that I'd hated since I was ten. "Why is a young girl like you doing the cooking anyway?" she asked curiously. "Where is your mother?"

The questions annoyed me, as they always did. "She's still in Syria," I mumbled.

I braced myself for the usual pity. But this time, what I got was a kind of knowing sympathy. The other ladies nodded.

"My husband is still in Syria," one said.

"So are my three sons."

"So are my parents and brothers and sisters."

I looked at their sad faces and guessed at the pain that

hid just behind the laughter that had filled the kitchen moments before. They didn't care about the circumstances that separated members of my family. They only knew that separation hurt.

We were all missing someone. . . .

Chapter 20

I don't remember how many nights we'd spent in Zaatari when the sounds woke me up for the first time. There was scuffling as something brushed up against the outside of the tent. Then I heard gnawing. Scampering. Scurrying. Scratching. Squeaking. Then I felt something right on top of my blanket. The squeaking got louder and closer, until it was only inches from my face. Then there was the sound of me, screaming at the top of my lungs. I probably woke up people in tents well past the two kitchens.

Dad fumbled for his cell phone and used part of its precious battery to shine it like a flashlight. It was the only light we had. He turned it on just in time for us to see a long, thin tail scamper its way out the tent.

Mice. And rats, too.

They became my enemies in the camp. If their creeping, crawling steps had remained outside the tent, I might have been disgusted but not scared. But the tent was not sealed, and they *could* crawl inside, so I felt both. We kept any food in tight containers, but still the mice came. It was not unusual for mice to crawl over us while we slept. Even when they didn't, I'd lie awake and think that they might.

Mice and rats topped my list of sources of suffering in the camp. But there would be many others. In summer, the heat was searing and the sun merciless. How I wished we had the shade of even one of our trees from back home! The inside of the tent was like an oven. During the day, flies buzzed around our food. At night, mosquitoes tormented me. I'd wake up with all sorts of bites.

Besides cold nights, winter would bring rains that turned the world of white into a planet of mud. Gravel roads became deep puddles. As hard as I tried, I couldn't avoid getting mud all over my shoes and jeans—and I did try hard, as laundry was my job. The water in the communal washrooms was icy cold. When I hand-washed our things, my hands would turn red and throb.

Then there were other daily worries. The tents were highly flammable. If one somehow caught fire, the whole thing would burn in minutes. And if a tent caught fire, the fire could spread from one tent to another until it burned down every tent in the vicinity. We worried about fires all the time.

Still, we learned how to adapt. The first time I tried to bathe with only a bucket of water, it took me hours. The fact that my hair was nearly down to my waist didn't help. So Dad cut my hair to shoulder length, which made it easier. I also got used to bathing less frequently, like everybody else.

There was only one challenge that I never quite learned how to manage. It was the one thing worse than mice: guilt.

Guilt is the hardest feeling for a homesick person, and I felt it all the time. For all of our hardships in the camp, we were safe. This gnawed at me like a mouse gnawed a sack of sugar. Why was I safe when kids in Syria were not?

My suffering was nothing compared to theirs. Those kids went to sleep each night not knowing if they'd wake up in the morning. I felt guilty for leaving rather than staying and sharing their suffering.

And thinking about kids in general was easier than thinking about the people I loved. Jadati and Aunt Zihriya. And Razi. And my mom . . .

I'd try to make myself feel better with logic. If I were there, would I actually be able to help? But knowing there was nothing I could do just made me feel more helpless.

People in the camp talked nonstop about what was happening in Syria. The bits of news that circulated told of a war that got worse and worse again. The idea that we'd be able to go home in ten days slipped slowly away. A month, maybe. Two? It was impossible to say.

We tried to gather all the information we could, but we were disconnected from the world. Cell phones served as our TVs, our movie theaters, and our newspapers. Most important, they were our only way of knowing if our family back home was still alive. But with no electricity in the camp, finding, and then getting time at, a mobile charging station was a big challenge. Most people saved their precious battery power by keeping their phones off and turning them on only in short bursts.

Our relatives in Syria sometimes had phone service and

sometimes did not. Sometimes they had no money. Sometimes they did, but it was too dangerous to go out to the store and purchase pay-as-you-go phone credits. Or they got to the store but there were no phone-credit cards, just like there was not much of anything else. We went long stretches without being able to communicate with them. During my whole former life, hardly a day had gone by without seeing my extended family. I'd never gone this long without hearing Jadati's voice or feeling Aunt Zihriya's hand on my shoulder. Being far from them left a hole in my heart that nothing could fill.

You could tell that everyone in the camp was struggling with similar feelings. Worry about family, and Syria in general, covered our lives in a layer of sorrow like the layer of dust that always clung to our tents and clothing. The difficulty of not knowing what was happening back home left us to imagine the worst, which made us even sadder and more anxious.

I did not live in Syria, but Syria lived in me.

Chapter 21

I was out walking with Mohammed and Tayyim one day when I saw a long line of people snaking from one of the distribution centers. People were lined up to pick up food baskets. There were people of all shapes and sizes, but everyone was equally tired and dusty. I heard the scuffle as some people stepped out of line to accuse others of jumping the queue.

"Refugees, stand in line against the wall," I heard an aid worker call out.

There was that word again, used with *that* tone. I turned my eyes from the scene, preferring to look at the sandy ground. I felt embarrassed, and also embarrassed that I felt embarrassed.

Most of the people from other countries who worked in the camp were wonderful. The teachers, volunteers, and aid workers made our lives better. Some would become my lifelong friends.

But sometimes, the way they said "the *refugees*" or "the *Syrians*" hit me like a punch. Their intentions were good, but the tone . . . It was as if we were lesser. Inferior or incapable. Like babies.

The truth is that we did need help. People had lost everything and couldn't stand up on their feet again without some assistance. But we had minds and skills. We were able to work. To think, learn, achieve, build, and create. There was a revolution because people wanted to live with dignity. Anything that denied Syrians their dignity did the same to me. Disrespect was the one thing that I refused to accept.

My very worst day in the camp was an encounter with disrespect. It was our day to pick up our food basket. Dad and Mohammed were both busy, so I was the only one available to go.

I took my place at the end of a long line outside a big tent. The sun was scorching and I dripped with sweat. As I waited, I heard the usual jumble of arguments from others in line.

"Hey, I was here first!"

"What do you think you're doing?"

The stress of what people had endured didn't always bring out the best in them. Some people fought over small things. I didn't get it. Here we were all equal. We had the same cup and the same spoon. Sometimes trucks came filled with jackets or T-shirts donated by some country or organization. Everyone would get one. All people, big and small, would then be dressed identically. No one could claim to be better than anyone else. Still, the arguments in line were a constant.

"No cutting!"

"That's my place!"

The sun kept beating down on us. The line moved so slowly that I wondered if it was moving at all. Finally I reached the tent. There I waited more. I was tired and thirsty. I wondered if I was going crazy.

"Syrians, stand in line!"

I kept waiting.

I'd spent almost the whole morning in line. Finally, it was my turn to enter the second tent, where they gave you your supplies. I stepped in that direction and a harsh voice shouted.

"You! Stop."

A volunteer pointed at me. I could hear that his accent was Syrian.

"But it's my turn," I said, flustered.

"No it's not. You don't go inside yet. Go stand over there."

"It is my turn," I said again firmly.

"I'll tell you when it's your turn," he snapped.

And at that moment I snapped, too. I wouldn't be ordered around.

Months of pressure had been piling up like dishes on a rickety old table. The table of my patience collapsed, and all my frustration came crashing down.

"Take your food basket!" I shouted. "I leave it for you."

Shock took over his face. He was stunned that a girl half his age would push back.

"I don't want *anything* from you," I kept shouting. I felt tears well up in my eyes and turned quickly toward the exit. I marched out with my head held high.

"Wait, wait!" I heard him running behind me.

But I'd had enough waiting.

I made it back into the sunlight and burst into tears. I can count on one hand the number of times that I have cried in public. This was one of them.

The man caught up with me and saw my tears.

"I'm sorry," he said. "I'm sorry."

I didn't answer him.

"Come back, get your basket," he said.

I wanted to refuse. But my family needed that food to survive. Was I going to let them go hungry because of my pride?

"Come on—you *are* next in line."

I followed him and took my place in line, but I didn't speak. And I did not forgive him.

Chapter 22

My camp routine began early: I woke with the sun, washed my face quickly with the cold water from the jug, put on my hijab, braved a trip to the latrines, and headed to the kitchen to prepare tea. I returned and laid out breakfast. When we finished, I carried the dirty dishes to the washroom.

I took a deep breath, as if I were diving into a freezing pool. I switched on the faucet and ran the plates and glasses through the icy stream as quickly as I could. I remembered how we used to tease Jadati for not rinsing all the soap off the dishes when she washed them. I now understood how years of washing in the desert had trained her to be sparing with water. I wished I could tell her that I was sorry. I wished I could tell her so many things.

I took the dishes back to our tent, set them aside to dry, and then walked over to Uncle Adnan's tent to visit Aunt Ayida. My male cousins weren't much help with her house-work, so I went by most mornings to give her a hand. We'd trade any fragments of news and kitchen news we'd heard the previous day.

"Good morning," I said one day, poking my head into her tent. Aunt Ayida was struggling to put breakfast on the tray while holding baby Emirate on her hip. I got out tiny bowls and filled them with oil, hummus, and that sesame brick that they called halva.

"Not like your breakfasts used to be," I said sullenly, remembering the jam that Aunt Ayida used to make from fresh figs from their trees.

Aunt Ayida managed a weak smile. "How are things over there between the two kitchens?" she asked, trying to shift the conversation. The grown-ups were trying to be strong for us. I was trying to be strong for my younger siblings. But sometimes it was hard to keep up a brave face.

"I miss Jadati and Aunt Zihriya," I heard myself say. I hadn't planned on saying it, but I couldn't keep it inside any longer. There were so many things I missed. Privacy. Real walls. Evenings on the roof. Trees. The sounds of birds. My teachers and classmates. But nothing compared to how much I missed Jadati and Aunt Zihriya.

Aunt Ayida gave me a soft look.

"I know. We all do."

We were quiet for several moments.

Then Aunt Ayida's tone changed. "I heard something yesterday in the kitchen that I think would be great for you," she said. "In the mosque, they're giving lessons in memorizing the Quran. It will give you something new to learn while you're waiting for school to begin. Maybe you and Tayyim can go over together and check it out."

The mosque was an extra-large tent. Outside, metal scaffolding hoisted big loudspeakers high in the air. The speakers broadcast the call to prayer five times a day, just as I'd heard my whole life. The mosque tent wasn't tall, and it didn't have elegant minarets like the one in Izraa. But it was a peaceful, spiritual, happy place, and the call to prayer sounded like home.

Tayyim and I had gone by a few days earlier to get information. Now I was beginning my first lesson. I got a copy of the Quran from the front of the tent. I kissed the binding and touched it to my forehead, a sign of love and respect that I'd learned from Jadati. I found a spot in the big open room and sat down cross-legged with the other girls.

The teacher called us to attention. "The Quran is the holy book that God revealed to the prophet Mohammed, peace be upon him," she said.

"Peace be upon him," we repeated.

"It consists of one hundred fourteen *surah*, or chapters. Each *surah* is divided into verses. We will go *surah* by *surah*. We will learn *tajweed*, which are rules for how to recite the Quran. Proper recitation requires precise pronunciation of every letter."

The opening *surah*, *Al-Fatiha*, was easy. Everyone knows that, because it's what you recite to yourself when you pray.

So the teacher directed us to open to chapter 78, *surah an-Naba*, or "The News."

Some girls started reciting to themselves, and others paired off with friends. I saw a girl who seemed to have come alone, like I had. I scooted over to her and put out my hand.

"Hi. My name is Muzoon. What's yours?" I asked.

"Hiba," she said softly.

She wore a long coat that we called a *manto*. I wore a *manto* when I went to mosque, but otherwise I wore jeans. Hiba, I'd learn, was from a more conservative family. She wore a *manto* every day.

"Would you like to read together?" I asked.

"Yes, that would be nice," she said, blushing. We opened our books and read in one voice:

In the name of God, the Gracious, the Merciful.
About what are they asking one another?
About the Great News,
About which they are in disagreement.
Nay! Soon they will come to know.
Then, nay! Soon they will come to know.

"Great, we have only a thousand more verses to go!" I said. Hiba smiled.

We continued reading and reciting. We'd each read a line and then try saying it back by memory. We both laughed when we made silly mistakes. When the lesson concluded, I asked Hiba if she wanted to walk home together. She nodded, and we exited the mosque side by side.

We were nearly exactly the same height, even though I was almost fifteen and she was going on fourteen. Hiba was quiet and gentle—a good balance to my fiery spirit. By the time we arrived at her caravan, we were fast friends.

Hiba means "gift" in Arabic. And Hiba was the first gift that the Zaatari camp gave to me.

Chapter 23

And so I added study back into my routine. I memorized chapters of the Quran in the same way I had always memorized lessons: by walking back and forth outside. Pacing between the two kitchens wasn't as nice as pacing under olive trees, but it did the trick. I recited *surah an-Naba* by heart without a mistake. The teacher gave me a certificate when I'd finished a whole chapter, and then I moved on to the next.

Hiba and I would go to the mosque together. Hiba also introduced me to another center that had activities for kids, like sewing and tennis. I asked the instructor there if they could teach us something useful instead, like English. He seemed a bit surprised by that but started writing down some English words for us. Hiba and I would take them home and try to memorize them, too.

And then finally came the day I'd been waiting for. The first day of school, at last!

In Syria, boys and girls were together in the same class.

In Jordan, girls were in one class and boys in another. The girls had the morning shift and the boys started at noon. I was placed in the ninth grade. If I studied hard through the summer, I could start tenth grade in the autumn and not fall behind.

I wasn't the only one starting school that day. Yousra came with me to the morning shift and went to the fifth-grade class. Zain would restart first grade during the afternoon shift, while Mohammed would be in eighth grade and Tayyim in seventh.

Even Dad was going back to school—he was going to work as a teacher during the boys' shift. This meant he would get a salary again. We had used up all our savings weeks ago. But soon we'd be able to buy vegetables and other groceries to supplement the food basket.

The classroom was like a tent, but with sides of metal rather than canvas. The first day we only did introductions. My teacher, Miss Miriam, told us about the subjects we'd be studying. Most were the same as in Syria. We would also have some new courses, like one on computers. But we didn't actually have computers, so I wasn't sure how that would work.

Miss Miriam was explaining that we would get books the following day when I heard the girls in the desk behind me begin to whisper.

"I don't need books, because I won't be staying in school," one voice said.

"Really? Me either," the other responded with a giggle.

I was confused. What did they mean?

Miss Miriam called our first day to a close. Everyone

gathered their backpacks and jackets. I swung around in my seat and locked eyes with the girls I'd overheard.

"Excuse me," I started. "Why aren't you staying in school?"

"I'm getting married soon," one said proudly. "I just came today to meet new friends."

"Me too," the other agreed.

"But what about your education?"

They both looked at me curiously.

"What's the point?" the first asked.

The second nodded, and they both headed out the door.

I walked home at a pace that was unusually slow for me. I just could not believe what I'd heard. Back in Syria, I never heard girls my age talk about dropping out of school and getting married. I didn't understand why it would be different in the camp. If anything, it seemed that school would be *more* important.

That evening, Uncle Adnan and Aunt Ayida came by our tent for a visit. Everyone was eager to share stories about our first day of school.

"Everything was great except one thing," I said when it was my turn. I told them about the girls in the row behind me.

My family was as surprised as I had been.

"Ninth grade is mandatory in Syria," Dad said. "It's unacceptable for kids to be dropping out."

"Education is preparation for the future." Uncle Adnan shrugged. "People are giving up on the future."

I thought about how Jadati would force us to go to school on mornings when we didn't want to. She'd remind us that she wished she had had the opportunity. "You should never

146

forget how lucky you are to be able to go to school," she'd say. "Don't ever take that for granted."

I decided to talk to those girls.

The next morning I slid into a desk in the front row. I hoped those two girls would come back at least one more day, so I could have a chance to talk to them. I was both nervous and relieved when they arrived.

I waited until recess and then approached them.

"You both are getting married soon?"

"Yes."

"Why?"

They looked at me, surprised.

"No really, why now?"

One of the girls sighed. "I have so many siblings, and my father is already struggling to feed them. It will lighten the pressure if I go to live with a husband."

The other nodded. "My mom is worried for my safety and says marriage will be my best protection."

I listened carefully. "I think marriage should be your choice," I said. "And if you want that, it's your right. But you can go to school, too."

They again looked at me like I was crazy. "Marriage is more important than education," one said.

"You don't have to choose—you can do both," I insisted. "Education makes you smarter and stronger."

I could tell they were listening, so I kept pushing. "Don't you care about Syria?"

"Of course!"

"Don't you want to go back and rebuild Syria?"

"Of course!"

"How can we do that if we don't have knowledge and skills?"

I could see they were thinking about it.

The teacher called the end of recess. The three of us headed back inside. I felt a burst of energy so strong that I practically skipped back to my desk.

Chapter 24

School continued and I made a new friend in my grade. Amara and I sat at the same desk and we started studying together. She was very smart, especially in math and science. Watching her do equations was like watching a soccer star make a goal. She just made it look easy.

"Do you want to be a doctor or an engineer?" I asked her one day when she aced our chemistry exam. "Or maybe both?" Amara shrugged modestly.

I'd aced the exam, too. In Syria, I'd been a good student. In Jordan, I was becoming a great student. I worked twice as hard as I ever had before. In the past, I studied for myself alone. Now I felt like I was studying for a whole country. Syria was in need, and this was the only way I could think of to serve it.

As the first days of school became weeks, I saw that there was no set number of students in class. Some days there were thirty girls and some days twenty. But most days there were no more than ten. A little fluctuation made sense. Families were always coming and going from Zaatari. They'd move back to Syria or go elsewhere in Jordan. Or maybe they'd just take their tent or caravan to another part of the camp. You'd meet someone and think she could become a friend, and the next day she'd disappear. Instability was the new normal.

But something else was happening, too. Many kids came to school just one or two days and didn't return. Later I'd see them in the streets or the washroom. They hadn't moved away. They'd just dropped out of school.

I started talking to girls during recess. I'd introduce myself and make the camp's version of polite small talk: "Where are you from?" "When did you get here?" Then I'd ask what I really wanted to know.

"What do you think of school?"

"It's fine for now," too many girls said. "But I don't think I'll stay long."

I tried to convince them to continue in school. I would tell them to believe in themselves and their capacity to achieve big things. I would say that in Syria, many schools were destroyed. There, kids wished they could learn but didn't have a chance. We were the lucky ones. The camp was safe. Schools were available and free. Didn't we owe it to the other kids to study? If kids like us didn't go to school, what kind of future could Syria have?

Some girls would listen, and others would not. Some were persuaded. Others brushed me aside. Successful conversations made me determined. Unsuccessful ones made me doubly determined. I had never believed in something so strongly.

I started talking to other people every chance I got. I spoke with kids on the street. I spoke to neighbors who sat outside their tents in the evenings. I'd go to the activities center with Hiba mostly to talk to the other girls about education. Many kids did not go to school but went to the activities center to hang out, do crafts, or play games. I'd find them there and try to convince them that school was the most important activity they could do.

I spoke with the women and girls in the kitchen when I prepared lunch each day. They'd blame the unfairness of the world for the hardships they faced.

"You're right," I would say. "But if we educate ourselves, maybe we can change things. Make them more fair."

"Impossible," some would respond.

I refused to believe that. *Refused!*

I became a one-girl campaign to encourage people not to give up on education—and not to give up on themselves.

One Thursday I walked straight to school without picking up Hiba. Hiba was the nicest girl you'd ever meet, but she was always running late and making me late, too. I wanted to get to school early because we had a math test. I was hoping to review with Amara before class, so we could help each other.

I waited for Amara outside the classroom until it was time to go inside. But she didn't come early. She didn't come at all. I felt alone with the whole desk to myself that day. And the next day, and the day after.

I started asking anyone I could think of about Amara. I didn't know where she lived and had no idea where to find her among the camp's tens of thousands of tents and caravans. We had no phones—no way to contact each other. I kept asking anyway. Finally a girl in my class recognized who I was talking about.

"Oh, her?" she said. "Amara got married."

I was stunned. We had spent so many hours studying together—how could she not tell me?

Then my shock mixed with such sadness. This was a girl with a great mind. She could have achieved great things. What future would Syria have if our most talented students were dropping out? I didn't want us to lose another girl like her. I became more determined still.

Chapter 25

At the end of one school day, Miss Miriam stopped me as I piled books into my backpack.

"Muzoon, there is someone here who would like to meet you." A tall man was beside her, smiling. "He speaks only English, so I will translate."

"Hello, Muzoon. I'm Toby, and I work for UNICEF." In the camp I'd learned that UNICEF, the United Nations Children's Fund, was the United Nations agency helping children around the world. UNICEF ran our school. All the kids got bright blue school backpacks with "UNICEF" written across them. That was the backpack I was wearing at that moment.

"I've been hearing about a girl on a crusade to convince people about the importance of education," Miss Miriam translated as he spoke. "I wanted to meet her. I worry she's doing our job better than we are." His voice was full of kindness and good cheer. He laughed, and so I did, too.

Toby continued. "UNICEF is working together with

another organization called Save the Children. We're hoping to find kids to work with us to encourage other kids to go to school. It sounds like you're already doing that, so I want to invite you to join us."

I didn't hesitate. "I'd love that," I said.

I joined about ten other girls at a training session later that week. We would be "peer educators" for what they were calling the Back to School campaign. The trainer told us that almost eighty percent of the kids in Zaatari were not going to school. *Eighty percent!* She explained that the two biggest challenges to education in the camp were early marriage and child labor. Families felt desperate. They were thinking about how to survive today, not about what would help their kids in the future. Some were giving up on the future altogether.

Another problem was that many kids had stopped going to school in Syria because of the war. They got used to being out of school. It was hard to get them to enroll again, even when they had the opportunity.

"There are schools here in the camp, but we can't just wait for students to arrive," the trainer said. "We have to go family to family and try to bring them back."

I was already doing this on my own, but the campaign would link my efforts to a bigger movement. I started immediately.

After school, I joined a staff member from UNICEF or Save the Children. I wore a UNICEF baseball hat over my hijab and a yellow Save the Children vest. We'd go all over the camp, talking to people. I'd tell them about the schools and the services they offered. If the family had school-age children who weren't going to school, I'd try to convince them that they should go.

People would listen to me because I was a resident of the camp, just like them. They knew I truly understood what their problems were. I'd talk to parents or kids or both. I never felt shy or afraid. Talking to people made me feel powerful. I felt the same surge of confidence that I used to feel when I recited poetry in front of the class in Syria. Sometimes I even remembered Abu al-Qassim al-Shabbi's words:

> *If, one day, a people desires to live, then fate will answer their call.*
> *And their night will then begin to fade, and their chains break and fall.*

I wanted to help break whatever chains were holding people back.

After one month working with UNICEF and Save the Children, I was getting to be an expert in education advocacy—including learning that what I'd been doing had a name! I did my best to answer everyone's questions.

"Why should we study here in camp? We're just going back to Syria."

What life will we be able to live in Syria if we are not educated? We need to invest in education now, while we can.

"I will send my kids back to school when we go back to Syria."

We don't know when we'll return. I hope it will be soon, but it might be years. What kind of future will kids have if they go years without school?

"Studying with the Jordanian curriculum won't help us back in Syria. The schools here don't give any recognized certificates or diplomas."

Education is more than a piece of paper. Knowledge is power, and it can always serve you. And if you study now, you'll be better prepared to get your diploma anywhere else.

"My kids are safest at home. I don't want them to get hurt at school or on the way there."

I worry about safety, too. But I can tell you that I go to this school every day and I feel safe. Being at school is probably safer than playing in the streets!

"I don't like school. I'm not good at it."

The more you go, the better you get. Give it another try. You'll remember that it can be fun.

"My son is working odd jobs to make money for our family. We need that to survive."

I understand. But without an education, he'll do those same jobs forever. If he studies, he can get better jobs and make a better life.

"Girls should stay home."

That is not what our religion says. Islam is a religion of learning and knowledge. As the Quran tells us, God's first word to the prophet Mohammed was the command "Read!" God's greatest gift to humans is our minds. It is shameful for us not to train our minds.

"I was eleven when the war started, and I had to drop out. Now I'm fourteen. I can't go back to sixth grade and sit with little kids. It's embarrassing."

Is not knowing how to read and write a better alternative? Everyone's lives have been disrupted. Everyone in school knows it's not your fault. And many other kids are in the same place. Don't worry about others anyway. Just focus on yourself and becoming the best that you can be.

Every conversation was a new challenge. I heard every concern and objection I could imagine. Each required me to develop a new response. It felt like I was searching inside a toolbox, choosing the right tool for the task and then putting it to work. But in this case the tools were ideas and arguments. Sometimes I revisited the same family two or three times. Sometimes it worked on the first try. Sometimes no amount of talking could convince people.

The campaign introduced me to all types of people. Some were wealthy enough to install their own kitchens or toilets in their caravans. Most were poor, and their tents were over-crowded with people. Some were optimistic and never lost their sense of humor. Others seemed defeated by their losses.

There were people who were elderly or ill. People in wheelchairs or on crutches, and people with special needs. Once, I entered a tent and saw a boy about Yousra's age, sit-ting on the mattress and covered in a blanket. I asked if he was going to school. He pulled away the blanket to reveal the stump of a leg.

"We were hiding underground during the bombing," he said. "I left to use the outhouse, and there was an explosion."

I tried to tell him that his mind was still strong. That he could still learn and that learning could give him purpose. I didn't convince him that day, but I hoped that I'd planted the idea in him like a seed. I hoped that other people might come after me and help it grow.

Entering all these different households, I saw one thing we all had in common. No family was whole. Many women had lost their husbands to war. Sometimes the husbands were fighting with armed groups in Syria. Sometimes they were in prison or dead. Or they'd been arrested and not heard from again, and no one *knew* if they were alive or dead.

Sometimes it was children who had died. In one caravan I found a woman dressed in black from head to toe.

"*As-salamu alaykum,*" I greeted her.

"*Wa alaykumu s-salam.*"

In the silence, I heard the echo on the metal walls as she

passed her thumb over her prayer beads and they tapped against each other, one by one.

Click, click, click.

"Auntie," I continued, "do you have any children?"

Click, click, click.

"I did, but they're dead."

Click, click, click.

Even if parents and kids were lucky enough to be together, there was no way the extended family was all in one place. As with us, some members were probably still in Syria. Others might be refugees in other countries. There was always someone missing. That's why you never saw complete happiness in the camp.

The people who had the hardest time moving forward were those from areas that were currently being bombed by planes and helicopters. Their thoughts were always with their hometown and the loved ones still there. Their fear was so constant that it was hard for them to look at life in any positive way.

As best I could, I tried to convince people to find hope in education and in themselves. This gave me a goal. And that goal transformed the camp for me. It was no longer just a place that I was waiting to leave. It became a place where I could make a difference.

That didn't make the camp home. Zaatari never stopped feeling like a temporary, unstable place. I thought about my family in Syria every day. We'd use Dad's precious phone credits to call Jadati, Aunt Zihriya, and Aunt Fatima. Usually we could not get through to anyone.

I never stopped hoping that I'd go back home. I'll continue to want that for as long as I live. But we never seriously pursued any plan to return to Syria. In our hearts, we knew that nothing good could come from going back. The idea of return existed only as a wish. It hovered in the air like a cloud of smoke. And like smoke, it evaporated gradually. We didn't even notice the moment it was no longer there.

PART VI

HOPE AND DESPAIR

July 2013

*We were used to life in the camp now. But not
settled. Never really settled. Some days brought
hope. Others despair. It was hard to get used to that.*

Chapter 26

I rushed into the tent and tossed my UNICEF hat and vest into the corner. I had gone right from school to do my shift with the Back to School campaign. Now it was almost two-thirty and I hadn't even gotten lunch started. Yousra was waiting at Aunt Ayida's tent, and she'd be upset that lunch was late again.

I looked at the food basket and weighed the familiar options quickly. Lentils and rice? Lentils and bulgur? Pasta? I still hated pasta, but it was the fastest. I grabbed the pot and went quickly to the kitchen.

What sounded like an orchestra of ladies' voices reached me before I even got to the door. I poked my head in and saw the kitchen filled with women cooking and not a single free burner. Bad luck. I went as quickly as I could to the other kitchen. Good luck! Free burners and only a few quiet women minding simmering pots.

I put the water on to boil and sank down on the steps to rest a bit. These few minutes, while waiting for food to cook, were my only moments to catch my breath. My days had become long and full. I had school in the morning and then went directly to work on the campaign. Then I'd rush home to prepare lunch for my siblings. In the afternoon I'd go to the activities center or the mosque, where I continued to memorize the Quran. I also did my homework and took care of laundry and washing the dishes. And I tried to help my siblings however they might need me.

Whenever I could, I practiced English. The international staff members in the camp tended to speak English with each other. I wanted to understand everything they were saying. I wanted to express myself, too. That motivated me to go beyond the English classes we had in school.

Many people looked at the camp as a place where life stood still while everyone waited for news. I wasn't waiting. When my head hit the pillow at night, I felt satisfied that I'd used every minute of the day productively. Everything I was doing was worthwhile. But I also felt exhausted. If I had a battery like a cell phone, you'd be able to track it going down, down, down, all day. By nightfall, I was on empty.

The pasta finished and my free time was up. I grabbed the pot and rushed back to the tent. The whole family was there, waiting.

I put the heaping pot of pasta in the middle of the floor and passed around forks.

"Eat," I encouraged them. They dug in eagerly, but I could tell they were irritated with me.

"My jeans are dirty," Yousra said after she'd eaten some forkfuls. "Are you ever going to do the wash?"

"This weekend, I promise," I said. "Eat more."

I was just fifteen, and it was really tough to have so much responsibility. But Dad was teaching full-time. Mohammed was working just as hard with his school and with running all over the camp to fetch water, bread, and the food basket. No one had it easy.

"Look at the little housewife," my neighbors would tease me as they saw me wringing laundry dry or sweeping sand out of the tent.

Sometimes I'd remember that, not very long ago, my only job was playing. Sometimes the pressure felt like more than I could bear. Then I'd remember Jadati and Aunt Zihriya and try to be strong in the way they would want me to. I'd often find support in parts of the Quran that we were studying in the mosque. *Surah al-Baqarah*, "The Cow," was the longest chapter in the entire Quran. When Hiba and I recited it together, there were a few verses that spoke directly to my heart.

> *We will certainly test you with some fear and hunger, and
>   some loss of possessions and lives and crops. But give
>   good news to the steadfast,*
> *Those who, when a calamity afflicts them, say, "To God
>   we belong, and to Him we will return,"*
> *Upon these are blessings and mercy from their Lord. These
>   are the guided ones.*

For sure, we Syrians were suffering calamities. Everyone responded in different ways. Some people were overwhelmed by disappointment. I saw how pain triggered hopelessness and despair. For me, this pain made me more mature. It forced me to become more independent and capable.

I was in a battle with the misery around me. I refused to allow these obstacles to defeat me. If life in the camp was a test, I was going to pass.

One day, a new kind of test appeared. I was in class and Noor, a woman from Save the Children, came in and asked my teacher if I could go with her for a bit.

She explained that a man and woman from UNICEF wanted to interview me. She'd already asked my father, who said it was fine, so I said it was fine, too.

"But why?" I asked.

"People have noticed how committed you are to the campaign," she explained. "We think you'd be a great representative to tell others about it."

Toby, whom I'd met before, arrived with a Jordanian woman named Zayn. They asked many questions!

Zayn translated for Toby. First he had basic questions about my life, family, and journey to Jordan. Then Toby shifted to my activities in the camp.

"What is your goal as an education activist?" he asked.

I paused. I hadn't thought of the word "activist" to describe myself before. But I liked the way it sounded.

I began slowly, but my words quickened as my excitement grew. "I want to encourage other kids to continue learning. I want them to be confident and trust in their abilities. Education is hope, and I want people to have hope."

He scribbled quickly in his notebook and moved on to the next question. "What would you like people to know about refugees?"

"I don't want people to know about refugees," I said.

He looked up from his notebook with confusion as my words were translated.

"I want them to *listen* to refugees. We have our own voices. People shouldn't just learn about us. They should learn *from* us."

Toby smiled and nodded thoughtfully.

Journalists came from all over the world to report on Zaatari. And now when they came, they would interview me, too. After a while, the interviews became normal. BBC, CNN, German radio . . . There were photographers, TV crews, and reporters with voice recorders and notebooks.

Delegations from international organizations or foreign governments visited the camp, too. Often I was invited to meet with the visitors. I would tell them about the challenges that children faced in the camp, and how we needed help to make sure every child became educated.

I welcomed each chance. I wanted to tell everyone about our lives here in the camp. I wanted them to know about our suffering, but also about our strength.

I talked and talked and talked. But it was hard to know if anyone was listening.

Chapter 27

It was a normal day at school in late August, and our new teacher, Miss Salima, was explaining an assignment. Suddenly the principal rushed into our classroom and whispered a few words in Miss Salima's ear.

"Girls, you'll need to remain at school after classes end today."

"Why? What's happened?"

"The situation is a bit unstable, and we don't want you to go outside."

"What happened?"

"What's going on?"

"What is it?"

So many girls asked the same questions all at once. I had a flashback to the times in Syria when they'd keep us late at school due to bombing.

Miss Salima's face showed that she really didn't want to talk about it, but we were hard to ignore.

"We've heard about a bombing in Syria. It seems that

the regime fired chemical weapons on the countryside near Damascus. We don't know anything more, but we'll tell you when we do."

Chemical weapons attack? I didn't even know what that meant, but it didn't sound good.

We waited in school for hours. I tried to read ahead in my English book and memorize some new words, but there was too much tension in the room. Many girls had families in the Damascus countryside. Finally the principal came back. She pulled Miss Salima out for a few minutes that seemed like hours. When she returned, her face was pale, like her body had walked through the door but left its blood behind.

"What happened?"

"What's going on?"

"What is it?"

Our chorus of questions began again. Miss Salima sank into her chair and began to talk.

"It was a massive attack. They're estimating that fourteen hundred people have been killed."

Gasps came over the room.

"Four hundred of them children."

One girl began to cry.

"Here in the camp, people are very angry. They're holding demonstrations down the main street of the souk. We think you should stay here a bit longer."

By the time they let us go home, the shops of the souk were closed and the streets were mostly empty.

Everyone was inside, watching the same videos again and again until cell phone batteries ran down. The videos we saw showed people coughing and suffocating from poisonous gas. Many were foaming at the mouth or struggling to breathe. Some had convulsions or muscle spasms. Others just lay on the hospital floor, their eyes glazed. Later, videos showed corpses in white body bags lined up in rows. Row upon row upon row.

In the camp, we had gotten used to shortages of everything. But that night, there was an ample supply of nightmares to go around.

Over the next few days, though, the mood of shock and mourning became replaced by hope. It was like a drop of liquid color in a glass of water. At first, a drop of hope seemed out of place. Then slowly it took over the full glass, giving everything its tint.

We heard that countries like the United States had promised to send help to end the war in Syria if the regime ever used chemical weapons.

For two years we'd had only bad news. So we embraced the news of this promise with both arms. The war would end and we'd all go home. Some people started making arrangements to return to Syria. A few families who had bought furniture sold it in preparation for leaving. There was so much excitement in the air, I was surprised to learn that anyone was upset.

"You won't believe how angry the shop owners are!" Mohammed said one day when he came back from buying vegetables in the souk.

"Why?" I asked. "We're going home."

"Exactly," he laughed. "They're fuming because they're going to lose the businesses they built in the camp!"

We all laughed at the crazy irony of it.

Anticipation mounted in the days that followed. Every day, I woke up and asked Dad the same question. "When are we going home?"

"Not yet," he'd reply.

As the days went by, people began to get nervous again.

New fragments of information circulated. America wasn't going to intervene.

Hope melted into disappointment, as it had so many times. But this felt different. Hope would never return with that same force again.

The world was telling Syrians that we were on our own.

Chapter 28

Sometimes I felt like my life was one of those snow globes. Revolution, bombings, and fleeing Syria set my life into snowy turmoil again and again. For people in Syria, the turmoil continued. But for me and my family, things had begun to feel still.

We'd been in Zaatari nearly eight months. We were safe. Dad could work, and his salary meant we were better off than most in the camp. We saved money each month and finally had enough to make a big purchase: a caravan! This doubled our living space. I was finally winning my battles against mice! We slept and ate in the caravan and kept our tent next door to store all our things.

The caravan kept us cooler during the worst of the summer heat. It also provided a more comfortable place to study when the school year began that fall. That was good, because it was an important year for me: the first year of high school, at last.

Things had settled into a routine. We all had school, and

chores, and I was working hard with Save the Children. So when Dad's phone rang one October day, I assumed it was another call from a journalist or an organization to interview me. That had become part of my routine, too. The agencies always called Dad to get his approval and make arrangements.

But this call was different. Dad's face showed a strange mix of emotions. He looked confused, sad, worried, and a bit hopeful all at the same time. His words revealed nothing. It was all "I see," "Understood," "Okay," "Understood," "Yes," and "Okay."

Mohammed and I switched between watching him and looking at each other. We tried to figure out what was going on. Finally Dad hung up the phone. He let out a long, deep sigh.

"That was your uncle calling from Syria," he said slowly. Arabic has different words for paternal and maternal uncles and aunts. So the meaning came through clearly: it was Mom's brother.

"The army has intensified its attacks on your mother's village. They've all fled and are looking for a safe place to live."

"And?" Mohammed and I said together.

"He asked if she could come here."

"And?" Mohammed and I said, again.

"I said yes," he said tiredly. "Honestly, I'm worried. I don't want to go back to all the arguing. But your mother has nowhere to go. I can't have that on my conscience."

Mom! I loved and missed her. I worried about her so much with the bombing in Syria. I was happy to think that we'd get to be with her every day. But I was nervous, too. It had taken a long time for the snow in the snow globe of our lives to feel settled. Now it was getting shaken up anew.

All five of us were anxious as we waited for Mom to make her way to us. Months ago, Jordan had closed the border where we had crossed. Now anyone trying to get out of southern Syria had to travel about two hundred miles eastward. They had to trek through the desert and areas with shooting and bombing. It could take weeks to reach the border. And once there, people often had to wait for many days before they were allowed to cross.

My mother made that long and dangerous journey. She arrived at Zaatari on a starry October night. Dad went to the reception hall to get her. When they came back to the caravan, I tried not to show how shocked I was. Mom was horribly thin and clearly exhausted. She had experienced war in a way that we had been spared.

Mom was desperate to sleep, so our reunion was delayed a bit longer still. But the next day we sat and talked together. We caught her up on our lives, and she told us about what she had endured. Her tiny village had been bombed over and over and over. Most of the buildings had been destroyed, and many people had been either arrested or killed. One of her brothers—my uncle—was dead. My cousin had been hit in the head by shrapnel from a bomb that exploded nearby and died instantly. She was just eleven years old.

Mom had witnessed these horrors and could easily have been killed herself. I knew that, but somehow hearing her tell it all in her own voice made it more real. She had survived, but all her losses had taken a toll. She was our mom, but she was changed.

The beginning was hard. It was a big upheaval for all of us. But day by day Mom got used to the camp, and we got used to having her with us. As she regained her strength, she began taking on some of the chores that had fallen to Mohammed and me. Before long, she was doing all the cooking and cleaning. She also fetched the water, bread, and food basket.

That meant I had more time for my studies and for Save the Children. And Mohammed had more time for school and for soccer and for building things with his friends.

Dad and Mom had all the differences that they had always had. But now we were in a foreign country, together in a small caravan, in a camp enclosed by a fence. We could not leave, and we had to make it work. So we did.

The snow in the globe of our lives had been thrown up in the air again. But it came down gently. And once it did, I felt more stability than I had in a very long time.

Chapter 29

Winter came. There was no heater in school. I'd wear layers of clothing and a coat over my uniform. Sometimes we couldn't think about anything besides how cold we were.

Still, I kept working on the campaign to encourage kids to go to school. New people arrived every day. There were always more people to talk to. And I was becoming good friends with my older colleagues in UNICEF and Save the Children. One afternoon Zayn came to see me in the caravan.

"A girl is visiting Jordan next week, and she'll be coming to the camp," she said, excitement in her voice. "She is an education activist and has heard about you. She'd like to meet you."

"Of course—no problem," I said.

I didn't know why Zayn was so excited, but didn't think much about it. That Sunday, Zayn and Toby pulled me aside again. "For security reasons, we haven't been able to give you details about the girl visiting tomorrow," Zayn said. "But now we can."

She took a deep breath and blurted, "It's Malala Yousafzai!"

They were clearly waiting for me to express my excitement. But I had no idea what they were talking about.

"Who?"

"Malala! The famous Pakistani activist for girls' education?" said Zayn.

"Malala? Who has been called the most famous teenager in the world?" said Toby.

I shook my head.

I had never heard of Malala. She had become a household name in 2012. We were in the middle of war in Syria at that time, and then just beginning our life in the camp. We could barely keep in touch with our relatives, or find news about Syria. News of the rest of the world was rare. The story of Malala was one of many that I'd missed.

Early the next morning, Malala arrived with a big delegation. She was accompanied by her father, security guards, representatives of international organizations, and other official figures. They arrived at our caravan in several cars. Journalists, photographers, and cameramen were just behind. As Malala stepped out of the car, reporters threw out questions like balls, hoping she would catch one and respond. The cameras clicked so fast, it sounded like popcorn popping.

Malala and her father entered and sat on one mattress. Dad and I sat on another. I spoke in English as best I could but mostly relied on the translator who accompanied Malala during her travels.

We exchanged stories, and our smiles widened as we discovered the things we had in common. Malala was just nine months older than I was. We were both the firstborn in our families. Our fathers were teachers who believed that girls should have the same opportunities as boys. Our childhoods had been disrupted by violence. We had both had to flee our homes and live in countries not our own. We both loved school. We both transformed that love of school into a larger campaign to make sure others had access to education, too.

We also discovered important differences. They made me realize how much I had to learn from her. Malala was from an area of Pakistan that had become occupied by the Taliban, a militant fundamentalist group from neighboring Afghanistan. The Taliban destroyed schools and prohibited girls from studying. Malala began speaking out for everyone's right to education. She received death threats but kept speaking anyway.

One day she was riding the bus home after taking an exam. A Taliban gunman came on board. "Which one of you is Malala?" he shouted. He identified her and opened fire. A bullet passed from the side of her eye through her head and into her spinal cord.

She was just fifteen years old.

"I woke up ten days later in England," Malala told me. She had been airlifted from one hospital to another. She underwent hours of surgery, including an operation that removed part of her skull. More surgeries and months of physiotherapy followed.

And still Malala kept speaking out about education.

I was amazed by her strength. Her activism brought her to the verge of death, but she persisted. I thought about my struggles with mice and harsh weather. Malala's suffering made my worries seem small.

As Malala spoke, I realized what made her famous. It was not all the world leaders who praised her. It was not the universities and international forums that invited her to give speeches. It was that she never gave up. She had a message and a mission. Not even a bullet to the head could stop her.

"This is a very happy day," I told my new friend with a grin. "I've finally met a girl even more stubborn than me."

We sat and talked. We left the caravan and walked and talked. People followed us outside, and after a while they asked where we were going.

Malala and I looked at each other and laughed "Nowhere." We just wanted to keep talking.

Then we piled into Malala's car and drove to my school.

"Everyone, this is Malala," I said, introducing her to my surprised teacher and classmates. I recapped her story for them in quick Arabic. Then Malala sat politely with us through math class. When that finished, she said a few words to the class.

"You can be anything you want to be," she said. "If anyone tells you differently, show them that they're wrong. Believe in yourself. Have confidence in yourself. You are capable of great things."

I felt Malala's words like a bolt of energy to my heart

and mind. I didn't want her to stop. I had been working for nearly eight months to try to inspire others. Now someone was inspiring me.

I joined Malala on her visits to other spots in the camp. And my father accompanied hers—they felt a great connection as well.

Before she had to go, I asked Malala to sign my memory book. It was the only thing I had brought with me from Syria besides my textbooks. I flipped past the messages written by my classmates in Syria, back when I never thought that I'd leave them. I opened the book to a clean page. Malala wrote in neat English lettering:

> Dear Muzoon,
>
> You are a very brilliant girl. I have not seen such a confident, brave, and beautiful girl. Your love for education is amazing.
> Believe in yourself, your potential, and your talent.
> Trust yourself!
>
> Good wishes and prayers,
> Malala

I was very touched, but what I noticed most was her beautiful handwriting! I had to admit that my handwriting was very bad. She signed a copy of her own book for me as well. We shared a long hug, and then all too soon she was on her way. The gaggle of guards and organizers followed a few steps behind. I watched the entourage of cars as they exited the gate and disappeared into the desert evening.

Nida, who had accompanied us as a camp translator, watched me as I watched the gate.

"This will not be the last time you two are together," she said to me, as if she could read my thoughts. "It's more than a feeling. I know that you'll meet again."

That day I realized that even if I left this camp eventually, my mission wouldn't have to stop at the gates. I wanted to make a difference in the world. Malala gave me a model of what it meant to be unstoppable. I was going to be unstoppable, too.

Chapter 30

After Malala's visit, even more journalists and TV cameras came, and it seemed like they always asked to interview me. I chatted with the UNICEF staff about it one afternoon while I was in the office after my shift.

"Do you know that journalists are referring to you as the 'Malala of Zaatari'?" Toby asked.

"Some organizations call you the 'Malala of Syria,'" Zayn added.

They both laughed. I started to speak but didn't know what to say. And that didn't happen very often.

It was an honor to be compared to someone who had accomplished so much at such a young age. And I'd felt an immediate connection to Malala. I felt like I had made a friend for life.

But . . . I was Muzoon. I had my own story.

Toby and Zayn noticed my silence. "Is something wrong?" Toby asked.

"No, nothing." I spoke in a quiet tone I didn't recognize as my own. I managed a smile and said my goodbyes.

On the walk home I tried to think through my reaction. I'd always thought confidence was one of my greatest strengths. And somehow being compared to someone else made me doubt my own path. I only wanted to compare myself to myself: where I started, where I was now, and how much further I could go. That was the comparison that really mattered to me.

And then I thought about my family. I knew they were all proud of me, and they were really supportive of the work I was doing. But I thought about how Mohammed must feel when teachers asked him why he wasn't as good a student as his older sister. Or how Yousra felt when someone called her Muzoon by mistake. I was learning these new things, too.

I decided that I needed to work harder to learn English. I didn't like it when people were speaking all around me and I couldn't follow what they were saying. I wanted to listen and understand. And I wanted to speak and be understood. I had only my voice—I needed to use it well.

I thought about all the translators who assisted the foreign visitors. They were all native Arabic speakers like me. They had worked on themselves and learned English. If they were able to do it, so could I.

In my English books, I'd circle words that I didn't know and ask my teachers to explain them to me.

I started to use English at home, just to practice. It didn't matter that no one understood me.

"Where is my dad?" I asked Mom in English when I came back to the caravan.

"Can I have more bread, please?" I pronounced carefully over lunch. My siblings looked at me like I was an alien.

But in each interview, I started to understand a little more and express myself a little better. I kept speaking, speaking, speaking. And my confidence grew.

Chapter 31

Things for me were getting better, but things in Zaatari were getting worse.

The first Syrians who fled to Jordan lived in towns and villages along with Jordanians. But as the violence got worse in Syria, and the refugees kept coming, the Jordanian government and UNHCR had opened the Zaatari camp and started transferring all new refugees there. The camp was spread out over about two square miles of desert some eight miles from the Syrian border. People thought it would be a temporary solution, just to give Syrians someplace to stay until the war ended.

But the war went on and on, more and more people came, and the population of the Zaatari camp eventually reached 120,000. That made it the fourth-largest town in Jordan, the largest refugee camp in the Middle East, and the second largest in the world.

It was an enormous number of people crowded into a small space. An enormous number of people dealing with loss, who often felt lost and confused and forgotten. There was no quiet, no calm, and no privacy. And the mice, shortages, and harsh weather didn't help.

People got into big fights over little things. There were some Jordanian police in the camp, but not enough. Residents felt like they were on their own to protect themselves, so they turned to their relatives. This made small arguments escalate into larger ones. Two people would get in a fight. Then their families would get involved. And then their extended families. And then sometimes entire towns or villages would mobilize on one side or the other. Conflicts sometimes destroyed tents or caravans.

Once, clashes broke out close to our caravan. The police officers threw tear gas. Then a man used a slingshot to throw stones at the police officers. One of the officers shot him in return.

My family scattered for a few days, finding refuge with friends. Yousra and I stayed with Hiba and her family. Later we moved our caravan to another part of the camp that seemed safer.

But there were fights there, too. One day I was in the caravan watching from the window. People were screaming— something was brewing.

"Muzoon, can you help me with my math homework?" Yousra asked.

"This isn't the time for math! There's a battle going on outside."

"Muzoon, what is 45 percent of 720? I don't understand."

I ignored her and kept looking. I saw people running and

fighting—lots of people were yelling at each other, screaming, but I couldn't make sense of what it was about.

"Muzoon, can you help me, please?"

"Fine!" I took a last look out the window and then sat
down in the far corner with Yousra. I had hardly looked at
her book when *BOOM!*

A stone came crashing through our window. The glass
shattered, and shards flew into the caravan. Yousra jumped
into my lap and we both screamed. If I hadn't stepped away,
my face would have been right in the path of that rock. If
Yousra hadn't chosen the corner as her favorite place to study,
she could have been pelted with broken glass, too.

Mom and Dad both rushed back to the caravan as soon
as they got word. Dad was very upset. "We never got hit by
bombs or bullets in Syria, and now we are hit by a flying rock
in Zaatari," he said angrily. "We can't live here anymore."

"Where can we go?" we asked.

"I don't know," he responded. "But we're leaving this
camp."

Dad had an older relative who had moved from Syria to Jordan decades ago. He was now a Jordanian citizen and lived
in town with his family. Dad got a permit for us to take a
one-month leave from Zaatari to visit him. Uncle Adnan got
permission for his family to go, too.

"We'll all go in early May, when school isn't in session," he
explained to us. "It will give us some time to figure out what
to do next. It will be like a vacation."

"Vacation! Yes!" Zain cheered.

I was less happy. What if we didn't come back? What about my education campaign? We were making a real impact in getting kids to come back to school, and I felt like there was still a lot more I could do. And what about Hiba? I saw her every day and couldn't imagine leaving her behind.

But once again we were packing our things—for a short trip. I put my memory book in the same bag I'd brought from Syria, along with some clothing and other things that I'd accumulated.

I still had the ninth-grade schoolbooks that I'd brought with me from Syria, but I was beyond them now, and it didn't make sense to take them with me for a month. We gave my books and a few other things to a friend of Dad's, who promised to keep them safe.

It was the strangest feeling to walk through the gates of Zaatari for the first time and get on a bus. We'd been here for fourteen months. It felt like a lifetime.

We spent the next month at our relatives' home, living as one family. Abu Euqla and his wife, Um Rafie, had many children, all of whom were married with children of their own, and they all lived close by. It was wonderful for us to stay in an actual house again. They had a garden with olive trees and rosebushes. We'd sit in the garden in the evenings. Their many children and other relatives came by, and we'd talk late into the night. It reminded us of being back in Syria.

And we were so close to Syria! Their town was right on the border. The closest mosque was in Syrian territory. We prayed according to its calls to prayer. Mohammed, Tayyim, and I would go for walks. Not far away was a hill, and when we climbed to the top, we got a clear view straight into Syria.

"We're breathing Syrian air!" Tayyim said gleefully.

We started climbing up the hill daily. But after a few weeks, we got restless. Compared to the busy pace of the camp, our lives at Abu Euqla's felt slow. It wasn't long before we'd had enough and wanted to go back to what had become normal life.

But I should have known—it's never as easy to go back as you think. And there is no normal for a refugee.

Uncle Adnan searched and found an apartment for his family in another town nearby. There were ten of them now, including active little kids. Abu Euqla insisted that they stay, but there just wasn't room for so many people at his house.

They were going to try living outside the camp. My oldest cousins were old enough to look for work, difficult as that was. It wasn't legal for Syrians to work in Jordan, but many did anyway. The wages were low and bosses often cheated them because they had no way to complain. But for Uncle Adnan's family, the opportunities were greater outside the camp than in.

They packed their things, and we shared an emotional goodbye. It was the first time in my life I wouldn't be living in walking distance from them. It had been a long time since I'd played soccer in the streets with Tayyim, but still—this felt like one more piece of my childhood, my family, my world, slipping away.

Dad started to investigate how we might move, too. When we were sitting under the olive trees one evening, he cleared his throat in the way he did before he said something that he'd been thinking about for a long time.

"Uncle," he said, addressing his relative with a term of respect, "I'd like to rent an apartment."

"Never. Impossible," Abu Euqla responded immediately. "I refuse to allow you to spend money on rent."

"Uncle, you are too generous, but—"

"Nonsense. You are family."

"We don't want to be a burden—"

"This is your home. You must stay here."

There was no negotiating. But I could see that it pained Dad to be dependent. We all felt embarrassed to be guests for so long.

Dad searched for other options. He learned that a second camp for Syrian refugees had just opened. It was called Azraq Camp.

"Where is it?" Mom asked.

"Far away," Dad responded.

"How far?"

"About fifty-six miles from the Syrian border."

I froze. That was much farther away than Zaatari was.

"What are people saying about it?" Mohammed asked.

"It's deep in the desert. Isolated from everything."

I could not imagine a place more isolated than Zaatari.

Dad caught my eye. "But it has a school."

I felt the tension in my shoulders relax. A school meant that I could move into eleventh grade. My siblings would keep studying. Dad would likely get a job as a teacher, which meant an income. For our family, a camp offered opportunities. And this new one should be safer than Zaatari.

Dad made calls to many different offices, and at last he got permission for us to move.

The day before we left Abu Euqla's house, Mohammed and I climbed the hill again to say goodbye to the border. We stretched our arms out wide to catch as much Syrian air as we could.

That's the closest I've been to my country in all the years since.

PART VII

BEGINNING AGAIN, AGAIN

June 2014

We were leaving again. With no time to prepare
or say goodbyes, again.

It was easier than leaving Syria, of course. But we
were moving even farther away from my country,
even farther away from my family, and that made
it harder, too.

Chapter 32

When we got back to Zaatari, we had only a few hours to say our goodbyes and gather our things before the bus would take us and another family to Azraq Camp.

I spent time with Hiba and also visited the friends I'd made at UNICEF and Save the Children. My parents and siblings visited their friends. As difficult as the camp had been, we'd built lives and relationships here. It was hard to leave the familiar and head into the unknown again.

I went to collect my schoolbooks from Dad's friend, only to find he no longer had them. He couldn't remember if he'd given them away or if they'd just gotten lost somehow.

I couldn't believe it! They were the things that had meant the most to me to bring from Syria. From home. And now they were gone, too. I miss them still.

My family's sadness hung on our faces as we boarded the bus. But the father of the other family was glowing with excitement. He laughed and joked. A wide smile didn't leave his face.

"I've never seen a person so happy in my entire life," Mom whispered.

"He must be an optimist," Dad responded. The name stuck. From then on, the six of us referred to him as *Al-mutafayil*: the Optimist.

Al-mutafayil was carrying a huge amount of luggage. It was as if he were transporting a lifetime of possessions rather than moving out of a tent or caravan. He had stacks of mattresses, bulging suitcases, and a stove.

"I can't wait to start cooking." He grinned.

Finally we couldn't hold our curiosity back any longer.

"Man, why are you so excited?" Dad asked.

The Optimist let out a hearty laugh and beat his heart twice with his fist. "My brothers and sisters and their families are living in that new camp," he said. "I haven't seen them in almost two years. Wherever we can be together is enough home for me."

That explained it. He was moving toward family, and we were getting farther away. I missed Jadati and Aunt Zihriya so much that I had to close my eyes. I didn't want to see the miles unfolding between us.

We arrived at the camp and were stunned to find a vast and empty desert. Zaatari had been buzzing with people, shops, bicycles, and noise. Azraq Camp was still, with a deep silence. There were only a few people. At night, not even a single candle cut the darkness. It felt like the end of the earth.

UNHCR had built Azraq when Zaatari became too

crowded. Eventually, all newly arriving refugees would be brought here, but we were among the first to move in.

"Village 3, Block 20, Street 11, Shelters 31 and 33," the man in the office told us after Dad had filled out a lot of paperwork.

"Excuse me?"

"Village 3, Block 20, Street 11, Shelters 31 and 33."

Dad looked at Mom and then back at the man.

"Your new address," the man said, pointing into the vast, open desert.

They gave us mattresses, blankets, water jugs, a tank of cooking gas, a stovetop burner, and some groceries such as rice and lentils.

A worker helped us get all our things into a car and then drove us to Village 3, Block 20, Street 11, Shelters 31 and 33.

We learned that a village consisted of several blocks. Each block had a few streets. Every street had twelve shelters on each side. The other shelters on our street were empty. Most other streets were the same.

"This place is a ghost town," Mohammed said.

"A ghost camp!" Yousra corrected him.

"And no pillows again," Zain noted. Again we cut a mattress to make our own.

As there were six of us, they had given us two shelters next to each other. The shelters were more spacious than the tents or caravans at Zaatari. They had doors that closed, which was nice. But there was no built-in floor—just a nylon mat to cover the rocky ground, so you could still feel the stones under your feet. And there was a gap of about five inches between the door and the dirt floor. That night I discovered that this made it easy for mice and rats to crawl right inside. Again—mice! And as Azraq was an open desert, it had more mice than I'd ever seen.

Zaatari had been pretty chaotic. People moved their tents and caravans wherever they wanted. Azraq, we would learn, was the opposite. There was hardly any detail that wasn't regulated. In Zaatari, guards looked the other way and let people go in and out. In Azraq, it was nearly impossible to get permission to exit. The security guards controlled Azraq with an iron grip.

"How nice to be in a police state again," Mohammed joked. "It reminds me of Syria."

Azraq remained a lonely and desolate place for a long time. Gradually, though, more families moved in. The camp filled with the sounds of children laughing, parents arguing, and neighbors exchanging stories. We stretched a piece of fabric between our two shelters like a canopy and would sit under its shade.

Finally a new family arrived on our street. Abu Hamza and Um Hamza had little kids and big hearts. They were from the city of Homs and had great senses of humor. Their family brought laughter to our street. Abu Hamza and Mohammed in particular became great friends. They could entertain each other with jokes and funny stories late into the night.

Abu Hamza and Um Hamza had actually lived in Azraq

Camp before us but escaped. They managed to live illegally in a town in Jordan for a while. But then police stopped Abu Hamza at one of the checkpoints they'd set up to see if Syrians had proper residency documents. Abu Hamza did not, so he and his family were sent back to the camp.

In Zaatari, most people had been from Dara'a Province, like us. They'd left after a year or two of violence, as we had. But Azraq was the destination for later refugees coming from all over Syria. Like Mom, these people had endured more of the war, and they had made far more difficult journeys to get to Jordan. Sometimes they waited under harsh conditions for months before a border crossing opened.

Each person who moved to the camp brought with them precious bits of news. Sitting under the canopy, they told us devastating stories. Some had seen neighbors crushed under flattened buildings or torn apart by bombs. They'd been forced to eat leaves and other plants when there was no food that they could find or afford. They'd watched the revolution evolve, with new groups emerging to take advantage of the conflict to push their own agendas.

Most people in Zaatari had faith that the war would end any day. Those arriving in Azraq were different. Given all they'd seen, they were convinced it would go on forever.

Chapter 33

When we arrived in Azraq, the camp managers gave us stamps to buy what we needed from a big grocery store that everyone called the Mall. They gave out twenty Jordanian dinars per person per month. Later they switched from stamps to a kind of credit card.

The problem was that that amount of money sustained people for only about ten days. If you were really frugal, you might make it fifteen days. People who did not have another source of income were in trouble. As we say in Arabic, they were living below zero.

I suppose the money might have been sufficient if the Mall had charged normal prices. But it was the only place to shop, and it exploited its monopoly. It would charge three or four times what stores outside the camp charged for the same thing.

The Mall employees would scowl at customers. Once, Mohammed took a photo of his friend in the Mall. Employees grabbed him and threatened to call the police. They were worried that he was taking photos of their prices to expose them.

We were lucky, because Dad was able to work as a teacher. He found work our second day in the camp, when he went out asking about schools for us. The official school would not begin until the fall. But UNICEF oversaw an informal school that offered supplementary lessons. An organization called Relief ran it. The Relief School needed new teachers badly. They hired Dad on the spot.

My siblings and I started going to the Relief School, too. It was good to have my mind occupied again.

And it was there that I met Razan. She told me all about the battles she had lived through in her hometown of Homs. Her family had been displaced many times and ended up living for a while in northern Syria, where a lot of people are Kurdish. She learned a lot of the Kurdish language and taught me some words. Then, after a few months, Razan's family left the camp. I never saw her again.

It was hard to maintain friendships when people came and went so often. But that made the friends who did last feel even more precious.

For me, that new precious friend was Rahaf. From the moment I introduced myself in the Relief Center, we clicked.

"Where are you from?"

"Dara'a Province."

"Me too!"

"How old are you?"

"Sixteen."

"Me too!"

"How many brothers and sisters do you have?"

"Two younger sisters."

"I'm the oldest in my family, too. It's a lot of responsibility."

"Isn't it? I have so much housework and am always taking care of my sisters."

"I totally understand. Me too!"

Rahaf and I had a lot in common. The more I got to know her, the more I appreciated her. She was very kind and sincere. Most of all, she was honest.

Before long, we were in and out of each other's shelters, becoming like members of each other's families. My mom had taken over many of the chores that I'd struggled with when we first arrived in Zaatari. In this new place, I had more time for studying and more time to explore with friends.

Rahaf and I would go to the various centers where they offered activities for kids. One center had arts and crafts classes, like painting or embroidery. I was terrible at any sort of art. I couldn't even draw a flower. But some of the other girls were really creative, and I enjoyed watching them work. Another center taught us about agriculture. We planted vegetables and herbs in wooden planters. The parsley flourished. But the tomatoes, eggplants, and green beans didn't take well to the desert weather.

We also went to a center that had computers that we could use.

"I haven't touched a computer since I was in Syria," Rahaf exclaimed when we went.

"Me neither," I said. It was a stretch to remember what I'd learned before we left.

Another center offered English classes. It repeated a lot of what I already knew but was better than nothing. I kept studying on my own anyway. I'd write words in Arabic that I wanted to learn in English, and Dad would give the paper to his colleague who was an English teacher. He'd return the list to me in English, sometimes with tips on how to pronounce difficult words. My English got better and better. Other girls would ask for help, and I tutored them.

Finally the official school year began, and Rahaf and I started eleventh grade together. Every day, we'd sit and study side by side. We motivated each other to do the best we could.

Just like in Zaatari, many of the girls who went to the activity centers did not go to school. I'd ask them about it when I saw them. They said they wanted to hang out with friends and do activities, but they weren't interested in formal education.

These girls had suffered through more upheaval than most people in Zaatari. Often they'd had to flee multiple times inside Syria. Schools were bombed, and it wasn't easy to find others still in session. Some hadn't been to school in more than two years. It just wasn't a part of their life anymore.

Some girls said that they wanted to get married soon. Many parents wanted that, too. They were depressed and afraid. They saw marriage as the best option to give their daughters secure futures. Even Rahaf's family wanted her to get married.

We were surrounded by many people who said that

education was irrelevant. But I encouraged Rahaf to follow her own path.

"You're too good a student to drop out," I'd tell her.

Her family didn't stop pressuring her about marriage. But they agreed she should still go to school with me.

I knew many girls were facing similar conversations with their families. So I started up conversations of my own.

I began in the Relief Center. I'd talk with the girls there about school and the importance of working to improve themselves. I'd go to all the other centers and talk to girls there, too. Eventually, that became my main reason for going to the centers.

In Zaatari, I'd gotten used to working with UNICEF and Save the Children. In Azraq, it was just me again—a one-girl campaign.

Before long, journalists got word of what I was doing. Then the calls and the interviews began again. Delegations and official visitors came to the camp, and I was often asked to tell these visitors about life in the camp and the issues facing children. As I learned more English, I did more speaking without a translator. I made all sorts of mistakes! But I was proud to use my own voice.

With this new media work came new problems.

"Don't be upset," Rahaf began as we walked home from school, "but I heard people talking about you yesterday."

"What did they say?" I asked, not thinking much of it.

"They said that you're only talking about education because you want to be famous."

"What?" I stopped in my tracks. "That's ridiculous!"

"I know."

"That's not true at all," I protested.

"Of course it's not. I know your intentions are pure."

Other rumors followed. Some people said that the only reason the media wanted to speak to me was because I spoke English.

"I heard about you," one boy said to me when I asked him why he was playing soccer instead of going to school.

"Oh, really?" I said jokingly.

"My dad told me to learn English. Then I can be famous like you."

I wasn't sure whether to be angry or simply laugh. I wasn't famous at all. My English was still really basic. And most important, I couldn't believe that people were missing the point of what I was trying to do.

Even some of the people working at the centers in the camp resented the attention I received. People said things like "Who does she think she is?" "The media should be interviewing us, not her."

This made me sad and confused.

"We're all working for the same goal. We should be on the same team," I said to Rahaf one day when I was feeling low.

"You're right," she comforted me. "They're just jealous."

"It's not a competition," I insisted.

"Don't let them bother you. Stay focused on your goal."

I was grateful to have a friend who understood me. The more people started whispering behind my back, the more Rahaf proved herself a true friend. What she said in front of you was the same thing she said when you weren't there. Her support meant the world to me—and strengthened my resolve to keep working.

Chapter 34

That fall we got exciting news: Malala had been awarded the Nobel Peace Prize for her activism. This is one of the greatest honors in the world. And Malala was the youngest person ever to receive it! I was so proud of my friend.

She invited me to travel to Oslo, Norway, to attend the ceremony. I was amazed and honored. But this was no easy thing. I'd never been anywhere besides Syria and Jordan. I'd never flown on an airplane. Like millions of refugees, I didn't have a passport and couldn't get one from my home country anymore.

Malala intervened and helped me to get a special travel document from the International Red Cross. It was a long and complicated process. They made arrangements for Dad and a UNHCR staff member to travel with me. We didn't say a word to anyone in Azraq. I didn't want any more gossip than I already had.

We had to leave the camp around midnight to make the long drive to the airport in Amman, Jordan's capital city.

"The taxi will be here any minute," Dad whispered when it was time to go. I followed him out of the shelter, then suddenly turned back. My siblings were fast asleep. I leaned over Yousra and said goodbye with a kiss to her forehead.

Her eyes opened. "You're crying," she said in surprise.

I was surprised, too. It was rare for me to cry in front of others, even my sister.

Yousra looked at me for a few silent moments as if trying to figure out why I was sad. "It's okay. Don't be afraid of flying—it will be fine," she said.

I lowered my head, suddenly shy. "I'm not." But I didn't have time to explain.

For more than two years in Jordan, I had not gone one day without seeing Mohammed, Yousra, and Zain. We had gone from being a big family filled with aunts, uncles, and cousins to just our small family. This would be the first time I'd be separated from them, even for a short while.

I hugged Yousra tight. And then my mom. And then Dad and I were on our way.

"It's freezing here!" I said to Dad as we walked out of the airport. Norway in December was the coldest cold I had ever experienced. I didn't know that human beings could live in that kind of cold.

That was the first shock. The next shock was the dark. The sun rose around nine in the morning and set around three in the afternoon. As soon as the day began, it ended.

Other things were not shocks but nice surprises. I saw trees, cars, billboards, and tall buildings. Traffic lights, sidewalks, and parks. After so much time in the camp, even the simplest elements of city life were a wonder.

At the hotel I saw Malala again, and I met the rest of her family. I also got to know the other friends she had invited to the ceremony. There were Amina Yusuf from Nigeria, Shazia Ramzan and Kainat Riaz from Malala's hometown, and Kainat Soomro, also from Pakistan. We had breakfast together every morning and told each other about our lives. We were all striving for something—all focused on education and making things better wherever we were.

The ceremony was elegant. The hall was decorated with bright flowers. There were musical performances and speeches. Malala came to the podium to give her speech. "I am just a committed and even stubborn person who wants to see every child getting quality education," she said. "I have brought with me some of my sisters," she added, introducing each of us by name. When she got to me, she said, "My sixteen-year-old courageous sister, Muzoon from Syria, who now lives in Jordan as a refugee and goes from tent to tent encouraging girls and boys to learn."

She continued:

I am not a lone voice, I am many.
I am Malala. But I am also Shazia.
I am Kainat.
I am Kainat Soomro.

I am Muzoon.
I am Amina. . . .

And now, again, I found myself crying in public!

There were many important officials there, and journalists, too. Some of them wanted to interview me as well as Malala. It was an amazing four days in Oslo, but I was ready to go back to my family.

"Everyone in the camp is so proud of you!" Mom said as she greeted us.

Mom told me that the manager of the camp had set up a big screen to broadcast the Nobel ceremony live. Many residents of the camp gathered to watch.

"When Malala mentioned your name, everybody stood up," Yousra said, leaping to her feet to demonstrate. "They applauded and cheered for you."

"People pointed at us. They said, 'Those are her brothers, that's her sister,'" Zain added.

"Even the people who've been giving you a hard time were bragging about you," Mohammed said. "Everyone's been talking about this for days."

I was really glad to know that my family was proud, and that people in the camp were proud. But it didn't last long. Gossip began again.

"She's a fool for coming back here," people started saying. "Why didn't she stay in Europe?"

I knew that most European countries offer something

called asylum for people in danger in their home countries. It's like another way of being a refugee. If you could make it to Europe or North America, you could request asylum as a way of staying there. Many refugees dreamed of living in Europe. People couldn't believe that I would travel all the way to Norway and then return.

I didn't understand those people at all! I went to Norway to support and honor Malala, not to seek opportunities for myself. And I would never leave my family. I wouldn't leave them when I had a chance to stay in Syria. And I certainly wouldn't leave them in Jordan now.

Besides, I was doing something important in the camp. Thousands of kids were still not in school. There was a lot more work to do.

Chapter 35

Life in a refugee camp will make you resourceful. Generators produced electricity for the camp's centers and administrative offices, while we residents lived mostly without it. But gradually, people came up with creative solutions. A family in another block built a windmill. They bent metal slats into something like a fan and hooked it up to an old car battery. It produced enough electricity to power some lights at night.

We got a car battery, too. Abu Hamza had started to work as a car mechanic in the camp. He brought home a used battery the garage no longer needed. Somehow he also got his hands on a TV and connected it to the battery. All the families in the neighborhood gathered to watch—at least until the battery stopped working.

Eventually, one of the organizations distributed small solar lamps. They would charge in the desert sun all day and then cut the darkness of night. The lamps also had USB plugs so we could charge our cell phones. Dad still had his phone, and now that we had a way to charge it, he got one for me, too. I created an account on Facebook and then WhatsApp. It felt amazing to be connected to the world. It worked well, as long as there was enough sun to charge. On cloudy winter days, we went back to no electricity at all.

People developed creative solutions to other problems, too. Mohammed and Abu Hamza took turns each day on water duty. One of them would make the long walk to the water tank and fill two large buckets, one for each family. It was a difficult task, as water is very heavy. So they set their minds on how to make a cart.

"Any old piece of wood can work as the base," Mohammed said as he thought through options. "But how are we going to get wheels?"

Dad responded the way he always did in such situations. *"Al-haja um al-ikhtira'a."*

"Yeah, yeah," Mohammed replied. "Necessity is the mother of invention."

One day Rafah and I came upon Mohammed and Abu Hamza tending a big fire. As we got closer, I was struck by a strange smell.

"What are you up to?" I asked.

"Melting old plastic jugs," Mohammed replied, as if that were a normal thing to do.

"What?"

They poured the molten liquid into four empty tuna fish cans. When the plastic cooled, the molded objects became little wheels. Mohammed and Abu Hamza fastened them to wood and made a cart to drag the daily water. Brilliant! Though—it turned out that the plastic wheels broke quickly. So they had to melt the plastic again and make new ones.

Another day I came home to find Mohammed and Abu Hamza piling scraps of metal into a big heap.

"What are you up to now?" I asked.

"We're making an oven!" Mohammed said, pulling his forearm across his brow to wipe the sweat away.

They had found pieces of abandoned metal scattered around the camp. But they needed to attach them to each other. The problem was that there were no screws to buy inside the camp. Again, Mohammed and Abu Hamza put their minds to thinking up a solution.

"We finally figured it out!" Mohammed exclaimed a few days later over lunch. Every shelter was held together by six screws. Mohammed and Abu Hamza experimented. They discovered that when they removed two screws, the shelter still held together with four.

"We're going to go to every shelter and ask for two screws until we get as many as we need to build the oven."

Mom rolled her eyes, as if to say that she'd believe it when she saw it.

But eventually they did it. It took two months, but at last it was ready. With metal and screws they created a dome-like structure and put one of our gas burners inside to heat it. Mom and Um Hamza baked cookies, pies, and pizzas. It worked just as well as our oven back home!

I put in a special request for *harissa*, and Um Hamza made it to perfection.

It was the most delicious thing I'd eaten in years. When I bit in, I thought of Aunt Zihriya and the *harissa* we'd made together. Then the sugar on my tongue mixed with sadness in my heart. And I understood the word "bittersweet" in a new way.

Sometime after my seventeenth birthday, Dad was making one of his regular attempts to phone my aunts in Syria. The good news was that the call got through. The bad news was what they told him.

Conditions in Izraa had been terrible the entire time we'd been in Jordan. But apparently things had gotten even worse. Our family had resisted leaving their homes for this long, but they finally decided that it was too dangerous to stay. They packed up whatever they could and fled to a different part of Dara'a, a region called al-Lajat. Everyone went together: Jadati, Aunt Zihriya, and also Aunt Fadiya and Uncle Suleiman and their children.

I remembered how people had come to Izraa when they had to leave other parts of Syria. Now my family in Izraa had been displaced as well.

They thought al-Lajat would be safer because it was under the Free Army's control. Also, it was a rugged, rocky area, and there were caves where they could hide from the bombing. And they *were* safe . . . for a few weeks. Then one night there was a brutal attack. People were sleeping when militias came into their homes and started shooting people at random.

Young men in the Free Syrian Army grabbed their weapons and tried to defend themselves. Many of them were killed, including my cousin Mohammed, one of Razi's older brothers.

I could hardly believe my cousin was gone. But so many people were being killed, it was also hard to believe that the others had managed to survive.

It seemed there was nowhere safe in Syria.

My worry for my family grew even more.

Chapter 36

That year, Ramadan came in June. Daylight lasted fourteen hours. Going without food was manageable. But we really suffered in the sun without water. Everyone's voice went hoarse. Our lips turned purple and cracked.

Still, we created as festive an atmosphere as we could. We'd stay up late talking and joking with our neighbors. At four in the morning we'd gather for *suhur*, a meal just before sunrise. Then we'd sleep late into the day and begin fasting again.

When Ramadan ended, my family got permits to leave the camp for four days to visit Abu Euqla in northern Jordan. We spent practically a full day traveling each way, but it made us extremely happy to see family. Especially when Uncle Adnan and his family arrived, too!

"Even the air smells different out here," Zain said gleefully.

I agreed.

It's funny how the camp only felt like a prison when you

left. As long as we were inside, we got used to it. I wondered if it was the same for our family in Syria. Even the most abnormal things, like war and death, become normal when you have no choice.

At Abu Euqla's we cooked a huge feast. Mohammed and Tayyim and I climbed up our favorite hill to get a clear view of Syria, and we breathed in the air as deeply as we could.

When we left, Um Rafie gave us some cuttings from a spider plant from their garden.

"Why don't you try to plant some in the camp?" she suggested.

"It's impossible for anything to grow there," Mom protested.

"Just try. A little green will do you good."

And sure enough, we planted it next to our shelter and it grew beautifully. It spread and thrived. Ours became the only shelter in Azraq surrounded by green.

In July, Malala visited Azraq. It was like being reunited with a family member. We held hands the whole time, like sisters. I could almost forget the contingent of security guards who accompanied her every step. She came to our shelter, and I took her to my school and the activity centers. By that time, my English had improved so much that I could speak about most things with her directly, but we had an interpreter just in case.

Malala was not our only guest that summer. One day, Yousra came home cradling a cat in her arms. "I found it on my way home from school. Can I keep it?" she asked Mom and Dad.

They both hesitated.

"Please, please, please?" Yousra begged. She loved animals and babies and any small thing she could take care of. It would break her heart to let the cat go. Mom and Dad agreed.

Yousra chose to name it Cat in English. She really loved it. She'd feed it bits of cheese or chicken. The director of one of the centers lived in town and also had cats. She sometimes brought some cat food from home to share.

Honestly, I wasn't a fan of animals. I was very afraid of dogs and I didn't like cats. No one else in the family was too fond of Cat, either. But Yousra loved her so much that no one could protest. Cat stayed with us for about two months. Then she wandered off and didn't come back. Yousra looked for her for weeks, but Cat was one more thing we lost.

Chapter 37

About a month after Malala's visit, the Relief School was preparing to move into a new building. There was going to be a grand opening of sorts, and they announced that the U.S. ambassador to Jordan would be there. It was a big opportunity for the school to showcase the work it had been doing. And this visit seemed to swell in importance each day.

Dad was still working at the Relief School. Saad, the school director, told him that the ambassador wanted to meet me.

"I'm sure Muzoon would be happy to meet her," Dad replied.

"We thought that Muzoon could deliver a welcoming speech," he said. "We'll tell her what to say."

"Excuse me?"

"We'll write the speech, and she can deliver it to the ambassador."

Dad hesitated. "She is free to decide, so I'll ask her," he said. "But I know my daughter. She'll want to speak for herself."

That afternoon, Dad told me what they had proposed.

"What?!" I said forcefully. "I won't read someone else's speech."

Dad laughed. "That's exactly what I told Saad."

"Even if my English isn't perfect, I need to speak for myself," I explained.

"I will let him know," Dad said.

Later that week Rahaf and I went to the Relief School for our regular lessons in math and science. Saad approached me as we left. I could see that he was mad.

"Why won't you give the speech at our event?" he asked me bluntly.

I answered just as bluntly. "I will happily give a speech. But I have my own thoughts, and my own voice—I won't let anyone else put words in my mouth." And then I added angrily, "I'm not a parrot."

Our eyes locked for several moments. His eyes narrowed. Mine did, too. He turned on his heel and disappeared into his office.

The encounter clung to me the whole walk home.

"They probably just want me to talk about how great their organization is," I said.

Rahaf nodded.

"I don't want to be used for someone else's agenda!" I continued.

"I understand," she assured me. "I'm proud of you for saying no."

I'd loved public speaking from the time I recited poetry in Syria. And maybe Relief's speech would be magnificent. But it wouldn't come from my heart.

A few days later I was at the Relief Center, as usual, and Saad stopped me again.

"We've chosen another boy to give a speech for the ambassador's visit."

"That's great," I said flatly.

He was trying to make me jealous. But it didn't work. The boy was free to make his own decisions. I had made mine.

Days passed and I put the event out of my mind. Then one afternoon I returned to the shelter to find Dad talking with two UNICEF staff members, Reem and Samir. I hadn't seen them since we'd all worked together in Zaatari. UNICEF staff rarely came to Azraq. I was excited to see them again and exchange updates.

Later Reem and Samir called and wanted to talk about the ambassador's visit, too.

Reem explained that the ambassador herself had asked to meet me. She'd heard about my activities and wanted me to be present.

"Would you reconsider participating?" Reem asked.

"It's an honor that she wants me to be there," I said slowly. "But I want to speak to her with my own words."

"We agree," Samir and Reem said together.

"And I don't want to represent Relief," I added.

"We understand. Would you speak on behalf of UNI-CEF?" they asked.

"Yes, that I will do."

At last the day came. The boy gave the speech that Relief had prepared. Then I met with the ambassador and just talked to her about what I thought were the most important issues for Syrian kids. We needed books, computers, electricity. We needed to be able to go outside the camp to pursue higher education. My words were simple, but they were my own.

Visitors were not coming to be impressed by fancy performances. They wanted to learn about refugees' lives. And the best way to do that was to listen to us directly.

Chapter 38

The ambassador's visit was the biggest story in the camp that summer, but in the wider world more important things were happening. New refugees were arriving at Azraq daily, and they brought news with them.

One evening in August, our family sat underneath our canopy with Abu Hamza's family and a married couple who had just come from Syria.

"Hundreds of thousands of refugees are sailing across the Mediterranean Sea from Turkey to Greece," the husband told us. "Then they walk across Europe seeking refuge in different countries."

"Smugglers crowd as many people as they can onto small rubber boats," his wife added.

"A lot of the boats break down in the middle of the sea," the husband continued. "They sink and people drown."

I felt so sad when I heard those stories. Some of the people making the dangerous journey were coming right from under the bombs in Syria. Others were refugees like us, living close to Syria in Jordan, Lebanon, Turkey, or Egypt. They couldn't cope with the difficult conditions any longer. They felt like they had no future where they were, so they were risking their lives in the hope things would be better somewhere else.

Stories of the refugee journeys to Europe were major news both in and out of the camp. Soon everyone was talking about them. People started trading information about how to get to Turkey and how much you had to pay a smuggler. They debated which country in Europe was best for making a new life.

I understood people's sense of desperation and longing. But this talk scared me. To risk your life at sea . . . I shuddered to think of it. The camp was not perfect, but it was safe. It had schools. An organization had started giving computer classes that could lead to an official certificate, a real work qualification. Rahaf and I were among the first to register.

I had no thoughts of leaving. Then a UNHCR representative contacted my family and suggested that we do an interview to be considered for resettlement in another country. We weren't sure what to do. We told them that we needed time to think about it.

Mom, Dad, and I discussed the pros and cons. We kept thinking. We kept discussing. I kept going to school and computer classes. I continued with my other activities. We thought some more. Leaving is always a hard decision to make.

I was in my last year of high school, and my goal was to go to college. There was no university in the camp, of course. It

225

might be possible for me to go to a university in Jordan, but it was extremely expensive and very few scholarships were available. The majority of Syrians in Jordan who wanted to go to university could not find a way to make that happen. And if I did manage to get a scholarship, I'd have to live far from my family. If my whole family left the camp together, that would be good for me. Would it be good for the rest of my family?

At the same time, the number of kids enrolled in school in Azraq was increasing. My campaign was working! It was satisfying to know I was making a difference here. But I now wondered if I could have a bigger impact from outside the camp. I might be able to reach an even larger number of people and tell them about our suffering and about our aspirations.

And resettlement—it meant we wouldn't be going back to Syria.

I *knew* we couldn't go back anytime soon. Hearing the stories of every new person in the camp made that clear. But to resettle somewhere else felt so final. Still . . .

"I think we should do the interview," I told Dad one day. "We can see what our options might be."

He nodded. That was what he thought, too.

The interview process was long. It began in the camp, with two UNHCR people interviewing my whole family together. Then they interviewed each of us individually. Then together again. They asked us so many questions. They wanted to know about every detail of our lives since birth.

Then there were more interviews in Amman. It seemed endless.

They told us that the greatest opportunity for refugees right now was to be resettled in Canada or Sweden. "Which would you prefer?" the UNHCR representative asked.

I paused to think about both options. If we went to Sweden, I'd need at least two or three years just to learn the Swedish language. This would mean a big delay for my university education.

If we went to Canada, we'd be very far away from Syria and the Arab world. And I'd heard the winter weather was really rough there. I really didn't like the cold.

There were a few moments of silence. "Which would you prefer?" the UNHCR representative asked again.

"Neither," I said.

He and Dad both raised their eyebrows as they looked at me.

"Excuse me?"

"Thank you to UNHCR for your help. Thank you to the Swedish government and Canadian government for their generosity toward refugees. But ..."

"But?"

"Neither is the best option."

"Is there anywhere you would like to go?"

I paused for another moment. "The United Kingdom," I said.

My main concern was continuing my education. I needed to go to an English-speaking country. But I couldn't imagine being an ocean away from Syria.

"The UK?" the UNHCR representative said with surprise. "But they're not taking refugees."

The determination must have shown on my face.

"We'll look into it and let you know," he said.

Weeks passed.

Then one day Dad's phone rang. He finished the call and brought the phone slowly from his ear to his lap. "Great Britain," he said.

"What?"

"Our application was approved. We have permission to move to the UK."

Before then, the UK had been accepting very, very few refugees. Then a three-year-old Syrian child named Alan Kurdi drowned while his family was making the boat journey to Europe. A photographer snapped a picture of his body washed up on a Turkish beach. The photo was shared all over the world and provoked an outpouring of sympathy. Suddenly people across the globe were asking if their countries could do more to help. Many governments decided to take in more refugees.

Great Britain was one of them. The prime minister announced that Britain would accept twenty thousand new refugees over a five-year period. We were among those offered places.

—

So. The option I'd requested was being offered to us. We had to make a choice now. Should we stay or go? What would life be like in Great Britain? What would we gain? What would we lose?

Most people would say there was no question. No one would prefer a shelter in the desert over the chance to start a new life in Britain.

But it wasn't that simple. We gathered for a family meeting.

Dad was the most in favor of migrating, and Mom was excited also. Mohammed was the most opposed. Yousra's views were close to Mohammed's but less adamant. Zain was still too little to participate. I had many worries but generally leaned toward going.

Dad and Mohammed led the debate. I listened, nodding, somehow agreeing with both of them.

"I'm thinking about your futures," Dad explained. "You'll all have greater opportunities for education and good jobs in the UK."

"We don't know that for sure," Mohammed protested. "It's going into the unknown."

"Perhaps, but I know that here in Jordan it will be almost impossible for you to work."

"But here we speak the language."

"You'll learn English."

"Enough to study in English? To work in English? That's going to be hard."

"It will be. But you're still young. You can do it."

"Here we have the same culture," Mohammed said. "Everyone is Muslim like us. I've heard they don't like Muslims in Europe."

"There is freedom of religion in Britain," my father countered. "We'll hold on to our culture and religion. We'll respect non-Muslims and they'll respect us."

"Here we have relatives close by. Abu Euqla, Uncle Adnan and Aunt Ayida. All our cousins. We have no family in Europe."

"We'll have each other."

"Here we have great friends. Our neighbors are like another family. In Britain, we know no one."

"Mohammed's right," Yousra interjected. "We'll be all alone there. I don't want to leave my friends."

"We'll meet new people," Dad responded. "You made new friends in Zaatari. You did it again in Azraq. You'll do it again in Britain."

"I'm tired of having to make new friends," Yousra said. "I don't want to move somewhere new all over again."

"I know it's scary," Dad comforted her. "But we have to think with our heads, not just our hearts. We have to do what's right for your futures."

Mohammed held his ground. His face showed the same determination he used to have when we played soccer as kids. And then, going for the goal, he put the most powerful argument on the table.

"Here we're close to Syria."

His words were like a soccer kick to the heart. Everyone went silent.

"Here you can smell the scent of Syria," he continued. This was an expression we used a lot, even though it wasn't literally true at Azraq as it was at Abu Euqla's house. "Britain is so far away. If we go there, does it mean that we'll never go back home?"

Dad struggled for words. This was the biggest fear for all of us.

"*Inshallah*," he said. "God willing. We'll return. The fighting will end and we'll go back home...."

Dad paused and we all waited.

"But that's not happening anytime soon. That's the reality. We need to go on with our lives. We can't just keep waiting. We have been given a rare opportunity. We have to take it."

Dad had made up his mind. Mohammed realized that the argument was lost. He tried one more tactic.

"Can we postpone?"

"It doesn't work that way." Dad shook his head "If we don't take this chance now, we might never get another."

It was decided. We were leaving again.

Chapter 39

I kept going to school until the last day. After all, what if the trip was canceled for some reason? Nothing was certain. I finished the computer class and got my certificate a few days before we left.

Meanwhile, travel arrangements began. We made a trip to Amman for medical tests and vaccinations. I joined Mom and Dad at a lecture put on by the International Organization for Migration to introduce refugees to life in the UK.

"Where will we live in London?" I asked the IOM staff member.

Since we'd applied for resettlement in the UK, I had just assumed that we were going to London. But that was wrong.

"No, you'll be living in a city called Newcastle. It's in the northeastern part of the country." I'd heard of the Newcastle soccer team but knew nothing more about it. I rolled this new word, "Newcastle," over in my mind.

"There's a good university there," she added with a smile.

I was happy and sad at the same time. I was excited about

starting a new life. I knew I needed to leave to continue my studies, and this way I'd have my whole family with me. But leaving the camp made my heart heavy.

We slowly began our goodbyes. Mohammed told Abu Hamza and Um Hamza. He was right—they had become like family to us. They took the news very hard.

"Block 20, Street 11 is not going to be the same without you," Abu Hamza said sadly.

"We'll miss you so much," Um Hamza added.

For me, the hardest thing was telling Rahaf. During my year and a half in Azraq, we'd become best friends. We were together every day and supported each other through hard times.

I dreaded having to tell her that I was leaving. Five days before our scheduled departure, I knew that I couldn't put it off any longer.

"What would you think if I moved away?" I asked.

"No way. You'd never do that," she responded without hesitation.

I felt my stomach knot. I couldn't bring myself to say more.

The next day, I plunged right in. "Rahaf," I said, "we're moving out of the camp." I didn't mention that we were also moving out of the country. That would be too much of a shock.

Rahaf's spirits plunged. She became awfully sad. We walked to her shelter and told the rest of her family, who had become like family to me as well. "How can we afford Muzoon's absence?" I remember her mom saying. It was crushing.

For the next three days, Rahaf hardly left my side. She'd stay at our shelter until night, and Mohammed and I would walk her home in the dark. Every time we looked at each other, we both cried.

The morning of our departure, she came to the shelter for a final goodbye. She had written me a long letter and gave it to me to keep in my memory book.

That book is the one thing I still have from Syria. I clutched it tightly as my family left the camp. Another journey into the unknown.

PART VIII

ARRIVAL

November 2015

Two years, eight months, and thirty days after we left Syria, we arrived in the United Kingdom.

For years we'd been leaving. Leaving Syria, leaving Zaatari, leaving Azraq, leaving our family, leaving friends, leaving so many pieces of ourselves behind.

I wanted this move to the UK to feel like an arrival. But in truth it took a long time to feel settled. It was a harder move than the others in so many ways. We were far from anything we knew. Could Newcastle ever feel like home?

Chapter 40

Our flight from Amman to Beirut was filled with other Syrian families who were also being resettled in the UK. In Lebanon, still more Syrian families got on board. We were a refugee express plane.

The trip felt unreal, just like our journey from Syria to Jordan had. We exited one world and entered another. We were strangers. We were tired.

We straggled off the plane and collected our luggage. A few Arabic-speaking women were waiting and greeted all of us. They checked our names off a list, and we boarded yet another bus. I watched buildings and cars and people go by and tried to imagine a time when it wouldn't feel so foreign and strange.

We arrived at the headquarters of an organization called New Homes, Newcastle. There another woman greeted us with a wide grin and a tap on her notebook.

"Hello, Almellehan family!" she exclaimed. "I'm Fiona. I'm your support worker, and I'll be helping you get settled."

She scanned our family until her eyes rested on me. "Are you Muzoon?"

I nodded.

"Your file says that you speak English. Can you translate for us?"

"I'll try," I said.

"Wonderful, love!" she said enthusiastically.

Fiona piled the six of us and our luggage into a van. We drove to a three-story apartment building, and she walked us up to the third floor.

"Welcome to your new apartment!" she exclaimed.

We stepped through the door shyly, as if we were guests of people we'd never met.

The apartment had everything we could ever imagine needing. There was a couch and a dining room table and chairs. The refrigerator and cabinets were stocked with food. The kitchen cupboards held pots, pans, dishes, cups, and silverware. The beds had crisp sheets, warm blankets, and fluffy pillows.

"Finally, real pillows!" Zain said with relief.

The bathroom was stocked with toiletries. Six new toothbrushes lay in their packages. I remembered our first months in Jordan and how I'd dreamed of shampoo and conditioner. I was thrilled to see plump bottles of both standing in the shower.

"Muzoon, tell her that this is too much," Dad instructed me. "We cannot accept so much generosity."

I turned to Fiona. "We can't . . . ," I began, struggling to find the words.

She waved away my worry with a flick of her notebook and her long blond hair. "This is just to get you started."

We had so many questions that we almost didn't know where to begin. So I began where I always did.

"Fiona, where is the school? When does it start?"

"In about a month, after Christmas, love. I'll take you there soon."

Chapter 41

Fiona came by nearly every day. She helped us fill out a mountain of paperwork: residency documents, health insurance applications, rental leases. She explained so many things: where to get a bus pass, how to pay gas and electricity bills, whom to call in case of emergency, how to use the post office. Everything was new to us.

We arrived in winter. We weren't used to this kind of cold, so we barely left the apartment for an entire month. In the camp, we'd lived our lives outdoors. We felt confined here in the UK.

When we did go outside, everything was a challenge: the culture, the climate, the traffic lights, the transit system. Dad took the bus once and rode miles past our apartment before he figured out that the driver only stopped when you pressed a button.

Little things shocked us. At the grocery store we searched for small cucumbers the length of a fist, which is what we had always eaten.

"They only have these," Mom said, holding up a cucumber nearly three times as long. We broke into laughter. Back home, we fed long cucumbers to farm animals.

On our third day, a man came to the door with a toolbox.

Dad answered the door and tried to speak to him in the few English words he knew. Then Dad called out to me in Arabic, "Muzoon, come help! I have no clue what this man is saying."

I quickly put on my headscarf and came to the door. "Hello, sir," I said.

"Areet, bonny lass. Ahm heeya to dee the internet," he said.

"Excuse me?" I asked.

"Whey aye, man. Ahm heeya for the internet," he repeated.

"What does he want?" Dad asked.

I shrugged. "I have no idea."

The man walked into the apartment and started inspecting the walls and outlets. He stopped in one corner for a while and started punching all sorts of things into his phone.

"Ahm gannin' oot for a bit. Be reet back," he said.

"What did he say?" Dad asked.

"Beats me." I shrugged again.

The man disappeared out the door and shut it behind him. I took off my scarf and plopped down on the couch. I'd been poring over my English books for years but couldn't understand a thing this man was saying. It was like he said all the words at the same time and swallowed half of them.

Ten minutes later there was another knock at the door. I scrambled to my room to fix my scarf. Again I heard Dad call out, "Muzoon! It's that man again."

"Hello?" I said when I got to the door.

"I got me tools. Giz a propa deek at that," he said, pointing at the corner he had just left.

He went back and poked around. He inserted some cables and wires and hooked up a small black square. When the lights started blinking, he thrust a clipboard toward Dad.

"Ye name heeya."

We looked at him blankly. He pointed at a form filled with clauses and subclauses and rules and agree-to-the-terms-here.

"I think you need to sign at the bottom," I told Dad. He did that, and the man disappeared out the door again.

I told Fiona about what had happened when she came that afternoon. She responded with a cheerful laugh. "Here in northeastern England, people call themselves Geordies. They speak with a special Geordie dialect. It's difficult to understand even for people from other parts of Britain, like me."

The worry must have shown on my face. Fiona gave another good-natured laugh. "Don't worry, love, you'll get used to it. You're just a new lassie in toon."

"A what?" I asked.

"A new girl in town."

We'd never been so far from Syria, and this made us miss it in a new way. I found myself thinking about home all the time.

All my life I'd relied on Dad for advice and support. But here he was relying on me. As I was the only one in my family who spoke English, I became the translator for everything.

Few of the other Syrians newly resettled in Newcastle knew any English at all. Soon everyone was calling me to help translate all sorts of things. Some things I understood, but everything was new for me, too.

There were many things that I liked about the UK. People stood patiently in line and arrived for appointments on time. Cars obeyed the speed limit. All the streets had names, and the map on your cell phone could guide you anywhere you wanted to go. The streets and sidewalks were clean. The electricity never cut out. The postal service amazed me. Offices said that they'd reply by mail. Within days, a letter arrived at your house.

Most people we met were friendly and generous. But some were suspicious of us as refugees, Arabs, and Muslims. We have an expression in Arabic: "Eyes can speak more loudly than mouths." Sometimes I felt people's eyes just a few moments longer and heavier than was normal. Maybe they were looking at my hijab. Or they were looking but trying to act like they weren't. Maybe they thought I was some sort of extremist.

What does what I wear on my head have to do with what is inside my mind? I couldn't understand why people made such a big deal of this. In Syria, some Muslims wore the hijab and others didn't. Most women in my family wore it, but one of my cousins didn't. So what?

I tried not to let this bother me. I was proud of my religion and who I was.

As hard as things were for me, I could tell that they were

harder for my parents. It was easier for us young people to learn the language and adapt to a new setting.

When things got rough, I remembered kids who were still under the threat of bombs in Syria. I reminded myself how lucky I was.

Chapter 42

Finally it was time for school.

Fiona went with me to get things arranged.

It was an eight-minute walk if you walked fast and hit all the green lights, or it could take up to twelve minutes if you walked slowly and got reds. I was learning to tell Newcastle time.

I couldn't wait for classes to start. During the war and then in both camps, school was my space of comfort and safety. School was something I could control when I had no control over anything else. It was where I succeeded when the world failed me.

But for the first time in my life, school was about to become a challenge to overcome.

"So you must be Muzoon. We've heard a lot about you," Mrs. Pearce said as Fiona and I settled into chairs in the principal's office. Mrs. Pearce was one of several principals overseeing different aspects of the school administration.

This was not the first time I'd heard those words, but something in her tone was different. It sounded like she was announcing the start of a fencing match.

"Thank you, Mrs. Pearce," I said. "I can't wait to start school. My goal is to go to university."

"Yes indeed," she said with a stare that was like the first thrust of her sword. "But let's not get ahead of ourselves. First you need to work more on your English language skills."

"I read and write English. I've been studying it for years."

Her stare stabbed back. "Yes indeed. But for *foreign* students the first priority is English."

"Foreign students?"

"Yes indeed. Immigrants. Visitors. Refugees. Those who are not British citizens need to learn English first."

It appeared that Mrs. Pearce was giving me my first English lesson. When Mrs. Pearce said it, "Yes indeed" meant "No."

"I was hoping to take regular classes with native English speakers," I said. I knew from all my conversations with journalists and visitors in the camp that the best way to learn a new language was simply to use it.

"Yes indeed. But we have classes especially for foreign students. There will be other Syrian refugees in your class, and you will be more comfortable there."

Another stab. Luckily, I was wearing protective gear. And I was armed, too.

"My goal is university," I repeated. I didn't want to study

English for its own sake. I wanted to use English to study other subjects.

"Then you must get the General Certificate of Secondary Education, or GCSE," she explained.

"What's that?"

"The equivalent of a secondary school diploma."

"Okay. And then university?"

"No, not yet. After you get your GCSE, you need to take three A levels."

"Pardon?"

"A levels are courses that relate to what you hope to study at the university. You need to take three and do well in each."

"And if I do, then what?"

"Then you can apply for university and see if you get accepted."

I paused to breathe in all the information. The system here was very different from what I was used to. And then Mrs. Pearce stabbed again.

"It won't be easy to pass all these exams. I don't want you to get disappointed. It's best not to get your hopes up too high."

"Yes indeed," I said, by which I meant the exact opposite. I was used to having high hopes. That was how I had survived the last three years. I was not going to give up now.

Chapter 43

Education in the UK felt like a hurdles race: GCSE courses, exams, A level courses, more exams. I'd have to jump over each of them to get to my goal at the finish line: university.

That spring I took GCSE courses in English and math. And media studies as an elective. Foreign students typically do a GCSE in their mother tongue, so I took Arabic as well. On Mrs. Pearce's recommendation, I also had some supplementary English-as-a-second-language classes with other Syrian students.

It took many students a full year to finish their GCSE. I set out to finish in a semester. I was moving from one school system to another, so I was older than most of my classmates. At first I felt embarrassed. But hadn't I spoken to hundreds of kids in the camps about exactly this? *Education is never shameful,* I thought, reminding myself of what I had always told them. I couldn't let pride get in the way of my goal.

English proved to be a challenge, but not in the way that I (or Mrs. Pearce) expected. I understood television and radio, and almost everything I read. But it was terribly difficult to understand people in Newcastle. They spoke so fast! The Geordie dialect baffled me. People pronounced English words in a totally different way here. And they had their own special words and expressions for nearly everything.

Once, my math teacher was handing back quizzes. "Eeeeh, A was stottin mad, me like," said the guy the next desk over.

He held up his paper to show me his grade. I guessed that he was upset?

Sometimes my teacher would explain things and I wouldn't understand at all. I started to doubt myself. I'd been really good at math in Jordan. Why was I having such difficulty now? Then I'd do my homework and realize that I'd already learned all this back in the camp. Math wasn't the challenge. Understanding math in Geordie was.

Mohammed was having an even tougher time. He missed our friends and neighbors in the camp.

"We have no one here to visit," he'd groan. "And people here don't visit each other in the same way anyway."

In Syria, friends and relatives stopped by every day. In the camp, it was the same. That was normal in our culture. We were always surrounded by people sharing food, coffee, and conversation. Customs in Britain were strange to us. People seemed to spend so much time alone. At night the streets were often empty. Even the streets of the camps had been more filled with life.

I missed my friends in the camp, too. I tried to keep in

touch with them through social media. Their electricity was limited, though, so we couldn't know when we'd hear from people. I looked forward to messages and calls from Rahaf most of all.

But things were changing for her, too.

"I want to tell you something. But I don't know how," she said during a call not long after we'd arrived.

I was alarmed. What could it be? I tried to stay calm.

"What is it? You can tell me anything."

"Well . . . I've gotten married."

What? I was so shocked, but I tried not to let her know. I didn't want her to feel that I would judge her or feel disappointed in her. I would never do that.

"Oh! Congratulations, Rahaf," I managed to say. "Are you happy? You are my friend forever! I just want you to be happy."

But really, I was sad that she had gotten married so young. And I wondered if my leaving the camp had played a part in sending her life on this new path.

"Yes, I am happy, Muzoon. And I'm still going to school— I insisted on that!"

I smiled. Rahaf was stronger than I realized.

"I am proud of you, my friend."

I studied every evening and weekend for weeks. In the spring and summer I took my GCSE exams and passed them all.

One major hurdle cleared! So now I set my sights on the next one: A levels.

When I was little, I dreamed of studying journalism in college. But after watching what unfurled in Syria, I had a new passion. I'd had to leave my country because of politics. My country was destroyed because of politics. I wanted to understand why this had happened and what I could do to help. I decided that in college I would study politics. I was excited to do A levels that could help me prepare for that. There were A level courses in politics, economics, and philosophy. Or maybe I should take history or sociology. So many good choices.

But it turned out I couldn't just enroll in the A levels of my choice. I had to get *permission* to enroll. And there was only one person who could give me permission.

"Hello, Mrs. Pearce," I said as I knocked on the door of her office.

She looked up from the big binder she was reading without saying a word.

"I'd like to talk to you about enrolling in A levels?"

Her eyes dropped down to the binder again. "No, I don't think it's the right time yet," she said.

"Excuse me?"

"Not yet."

"Can I ask why?"

"*May* you ask why?"

"May I ask why?"

"I'm afraid that you will fail."

"But, Mrs. Pearce, I've passed my GCSEs. Why do you think I will fail?"

"A level courses are harder."

251

"I just want a chance. Please at least give me a chance to fail."

"Do you think you know the British educational system better than I do?"

"No, Mrs. Pearce, of course not—"

"Then you shouldn't doubt my judgment."

"I'm sorry, I didn't mean to—"

"Be patient. I will let you know when the time is right."

I had no problem waiting. I just wanted to know that I was waiting for *something*. I needed to know that I was moving forward and not standing still. I reminded myself of *surah al-Baqarah. Life is filled with trials; if you're patient, you'll be rewarded in the end.*

I lowered my head and backed out of the office. But later that week I returned to ask again. And again. And again. And again. I asked her at least twice a week for more weeks than I can remember.

Finally at the end of summer, I got good news.

"I've decided to permit you to enroll in A level classes in September."

A wave of relief grew inside me.

"Photography, I think."

The wave came crashing down, and I found myself gasping for air. I wasn't interested in photography. I wanted something related to politics.

"Why that subject? It's not preparation for what I want to study in university."

"You're still improving your English. Photography is good for your level."

I controlled my anger. "And what will my other A levels be?"

"Arabic."

"Arabic?"

"Yes."

"I was hoping to learn something new. I've been studying Arabic my whole life."

"Well, you won't fail, then."

I couldn't understand why she was so focused on my failing. I took a deep breath and continued, "And what will my third A level course be?" I asked.

"I've decided that you should enroll only in two courses this year. Photography and Arabic."

"But I need three A levels to apply to university!" I protested.

"Yes indeed. Two are plenty for now. We can think about a third course later."

I felt lost. I was so new in this country. Maybe Mrs. Pearce was right. She surely understood things that I didn't. Besides, she was a teacher. I'd been raised to respect teachers. But something wasn't right. Mrs. Pearce doubted my abilities. That was making me doubt myself. Self-confidence had been my greatest power, and I felt it slipping away.

"I'm confused," I told Dad. "I don't know what to do."

Dad had already gone in to speak with Mrs. Pearce a few times. He was confused, too.

"Usually it's teachers who have to beg students to study," he said. "But in this case a student is begging the teacher for the chance to study!"

"She keeps telling me that I'll fail."

"That's not right," he said. "The only failure is fear of failure. The only failure is not trying."

"That's what I told her!" I said in frustration.

"I wish I could guide you better." Dad shook his head. I could tell he felt as bad as I did. He was struggling to understand the British educational system. He tried to read through all the paperwork that I brought home from the school. But everything was so different from what we were used to.

"I don't understand it," he said again. "But there's one thing I know: *Qalb el mu'men dalilu.*"

Dad had a proverb or verse of poetry for every occasion. This one meant "The heart of a true believer will show him the way."

"If you have faith, your heart will tell you what you need to do."

My heart was skeptical of Mrs. Pearce. But it told me to give her more time. *Be patient,* I reminded myself. *Good comes to those who are patient.*

Chapter 44

That school year I tried to make the most of the photography class. The Arabic course was not much of a course at all. Even the teacher recognized that it was not useful for me. Instead, she met with me from time to time and gave me some materials to look at in preparation for the exam.

I continued to stop by Mrs. Pearce's office and ask her when she would assign me a third A level course. She'd wave away my questions. "Later," she'd say. "When you're ready."

At school, I kept my eyes on the hurdles that stood between me and going to university. Meanwhile, other challenges kept us busy at home. I was studying my photography textbook one night when I was startled by the doorbell.

Buzz, buzz, buzz, buzz, buzz, buzz, buzz, buzz, buzz, buzz, buzz, buzz, buzz.

"Why are they doing this to us? What did we do to them?" Yousra moaned.

A gang of young guys in the neighborhood were harassing

us. They'd ring our bell twenty times in a row. Sometimes they threw rocks at our window.

The harassment was worse when we went on the street. They shouted angry words at Dad. We assumed they were swearing. I was glad that Dad didn't know enough English to understand the specifics.

This went on for months. Then one day Mohammed was walking to the grocery store. Guys from the gang followed him and started throwing rocks. One hit Mohammed on the head. Blood flowed as he ran home. We rushed him to the hospital, and police came to investigate the incident. They talked to Mohammed and later talked to the gang. The gang said that Mohammed had initiated a fight. The police wrote up a report that said that rocks were thrown in self-defense.

It was a lie, but there was nothing we could do about it.

We were all very upset around the dinner table that night.

"If I'd thrown rocks at them, they would have put me in jail for life!" Mohammed said, touching the stitches on his head.

As refugees, we felt that we always had to be on our best behavior. We couldn't make the slightest problem. But if other people made problems for us, we had to accept it.

"When people started throwing rocks in Zaatari, we found a new place to live. I think it's time to find a new place here now," Dad said.

Leaving again . . . it felt like a defeat.

But Zain found the silver lining: "Can we bring our pillows?"

We all laughed.

"Yes," my father said. "We can bring everything."

—

Dad found a new home for us in a better neighborhood, far away from the gang.

And this move *did* feel different. We knew what we needed now, and we knew how to find it.

In this safer neighborhood we began to settle in.

Mohammed brought home a spider plant that reminded all of us of the miraculous plants in Azraq.

And I found rose water and semolina in the grocery store—and *Manal Al-Alem's Kitchen* on YouTube—and made my first *harissa* in the UK.

It wasn't perfect, but it was more sweet than bitter.

Chapter 45

I tried to stay focused on my two missions at school: preparing to pass my photography and Arabic exams, and pestering Mrs. Pearce to enroll me in a third A level course.

I was also continuing my campaign for refugee education.

About a month after we'd arrived in Newcastle, Malala and her family came to visit us. They were living in Birmingham, about three hours away by car. Many other visits would bring our families even closer together. It turned out we *did* have friends in the UK!

When I talked to her, she asked me to become involved in the charitable organization that she and her family had founded to advance education for girls around the world. I happily agreed. I started attending conferences where I gave speeches and continued to talk to journalists. Each event led to invitations for new events. Former U.S. president Bill Clinton invited me to speak at the Clinton Foundation in New York. While I was there, I also spoke at meetings organized around the United Nations General Assembly. I got awards, including one naming me among the Arab women of the year.

I started speaking more about my personal story and the challenges that I'd faced as a refugee. "Refugees are ordinary people who have a lot to give but lack opportunities," I'd say. I'd encourage individuals and governments to do more to ensure refugees' access to education. Many times I was the youngest person in the room. But I was never afraid. I was filled with determination and passion, because I was representing something larger than myself.

I also kept in touch with my friends at UNICEF, which had had such an important impact on my life. UNICEF oversaw all the schools I'd attended in the camps. UNICEF was the first to recognize and support my activism. Its officers would follow my media appearances and reach out to me. When they saw that I was traveling outside the UK, they got to thinking. And in the spring, they reached out with an unexpected invitation.

"UNICEF is asking me to accompany them to Chad!" I shouted when I read the email.

"Who's that?" Zain asked.

"It's not a person, silly. It's a country—in Africa."

I immediately accepted. During the weeklong trip, I met women and children who had fled from Boko Haram, a violent extremist group in neighboring Nigeria. I met a sixteen-year-old girl named Hasima. Boko Haram had kidnapped her and 275 other girls from their school. They had tortured her, but she had managed to escape and was being treated in a UNICEF hospital.

"I want to go back to school," Hasima told me when I visited her in the hospital. "Education will make my future better than my past."

I will never forget our conversation. It is easy to have hope when life is good. But hope matters most when life is cruel and unfair. Finding hope then is an act of true courage. Hasima's bravery inspired me.

Not long after I returned from Chad, I received another email from UNICEF. They told me that they would like to appoint me a goodwill ambassador.

"What's a goodwill ambassador?" Mohammed asked.

I answered him, "They're like celebrities who make speeches and go on field visits to support UNICEF. They try to raise awareness about children's rights."

"Are you a celebrity?" Yousra asked.

"Well, I'm not a movie star," I laughed. "But I guess UNICEF thinks I have something to contribute to their mission."

I typed out an email saying that I was honored to accept. The next month, they announced my appointment in an official press release. I read it out loud to my family:

New York, 19 June 2017—UNICEF announced today, on the eve of World Refugee Day, the appointment of Muzoon Almellehan, a 19-year-old education activist and Syrian refugee, as its newest—and

I was traveling the world and speaking before diplomats and
heads of state. I was getting recognition from some of the
most important institutions in the world. But my biggest goal
remained going to university. And to achieve that, one hurdle
still stood in my way.

"Mrs. Pearce?" I asked as I knocked on her door.

She lifted her head from her binder.

"Have you decided when you will allow me to enroll in
a third A level?"

Her gaze went back to her binder. "During the next school
year," she replied.

"*Next year?*"

"Yes indeed."

I was more than frustrated. I was exasperated and angry
But this school year was more than half finished. Even if
Mrs. Pearce allowed me into a new class tomorrow, it would
be too far along for me to catch up.

"Could you tell me which course that will be? I'd like to
start preparing."

She gave me a long look. "I recommend religious studies
and ethics. I think that will suit you."

A week went by. I stopped by Mrs. Pearce's office again.

"Is everything set with religious studies and ethics for next year?"

"Oh, there is bad news," she said. "It turns out that that course is not offered next year after all."

I didn't understand. Did subjects run out? Like fresh bread at the bakery?

"Is there another course I can take?" I asked nervously.

"Be patient. I'll assess options soon."

Another few weeks passed. I continued to stop by Mrs. Pearce's office and ask about my third class. She told me that she would tell me later. Later would come and she'd tell me the same thing.

One day, she finally gave me a more definitive answer.

"I've decided not to assign you to a third class."

I was shocked.

"But you promised. . . ."

"Yes indeed. But I believe that you still need to work more on your English."

She'd been misleading me all along. And she wasn't *listening* to me. To what I needed. She was like the aid workers who thought they knew what refugees needed without actually listening to them.

"You can take the remainder of photography again," she said.

"No."

"What?"

"I'm leaving this school."

This was a leaving I could feel good about!

I had only my voice, and my determination not to give up. And I was using them.

I didn't know where I would go next, but I said to myself: *The heart of a true believer will show him the way.* My heart was telling me that I needed to move to another school. That I could find a principal who believed in me as I believed in myself. That I could not only pass my A levels but ace them. That I could achieve my goal of going to university.

Chapter 46

On September twenty-fourth, I hopped on a bus and passed familiar streets and shops.

My excitement grew as my stop approached. I stepped off the bus and hitched the backpack higher up on my shoulder. Then I walked through the gates of Newcastle University for the first time.

This was just an orientation day, so my backpack held only a notebook and some pens. But there would be new books to fill it soon. I would be studying history and politics and learning about how events shape the world. And about how I can help shape events. . . .

One of my first courses was called Order and Disorder, which I surely knew a lot about already. But I was eager to learn more. Always.

I'd come a very long way from the streets of Izraa. Survived more than twelve-year-old me could ever have imagined.

There would be new challenges ahead. Always.

But I was ready for them.

For the first time in a very long time, I felt like I had arrived.

Epilogue

As I write these words, I am now a college graduate. I chose to attend Newcastle University so I could live at home with my family.

Dad continues to take English classes daily. Mom also goes to English classes and has made a tight circle of new friends. Mohammed is studying English and computer science at college. Yousra is in year twelve, where she is taking chemistry, physics, and biology A levels. She's a top student and wants to be a doctor. Zain is fourteen, and his Geordie English is practically better than his Arabic. He's as obsessed with soccer as I was when I was his age.

Uncle Adnan and his family are still in Jordan. Mansour is working. Tayyim finished high school with good grades and is hoping to go to university. Uncle Adnan's health is not good. That has been difficult for all of us, and especially Dad, who aches being so far from his brother.

We stay in touch with our family in Syria as much as we can. Jadati is in her eighties and still amazes us with her strength. Aunt Zihriya stays by her side, also as strong as ever, and has retired from her job as a principal. They continue to be what I miss most about Syria.

Fighting goes on there still, but most of my family were able to go back to Izraa. When Aunt Zihriya returned to her apartment, she found that everything had been stolen. Forces loyal to the regime even took the doors and windows from their frames. When Aunt Fadiya returned to her house, she found that an army officer had moved in and made it his own.

Our house is okay, because another one of our relatives moved in after we left and kept an eye on it. Jadati and Aunt Zihriya live there now.

Shortly after they returned to Izraa, Dad's friend Abu Faysal stopped by to check on them. Dad had not spoken with him since we left—he worried that if he called Abu Faysal, it would get him in trouble. Now Dad could call Aunt Zihriya, and she put Abu Faysal on the line. They exchanged joyful greetings, but then Abu Faysal became upset.

"People have been entering your land and taking your olives and almonds," Abu Faysal said angrily. "When I see them, I remember the days we used to harvest together."

"Don't worry, my friend," Dad told him. "I am glad to know the trees survive. I am glad that you survive."

It is a comfort for me to be able to picture my relatives in our old house, among the olives and almonds....

Two of my older cousins were not allowed to go home. The government blocked Razi's older sister because she and her husband were media activists who had written criticism of the regime. They are refugees now. At first they were in

Turkey, but they have left there and we don't know where they are. Razi's brother Akram was a volunteer for the White Helmets, the crew of first responders that rushed to the scenes of bombings to rescue people from under collapsed buildings. He is now a refugee, too, in a place very far from home—it would not be safe to say where exactly. He's lonely by himself in such a different place, but trying to adapt. Razi, meanwhile, stays close to Aunt Fadiya's side. Sadly, Uncle Suleiman had cancer and died last year. He wasn't able to get proper treatment while they were being displaced from one town to another. The stress of everything, including the death of his son Mohammed, took a toll on him. On all of them, really.

Another sad loss: Hiba, my dear friend in the Zaatari camp, also had cancer. She, too, didn't get the kind of health care that might have led to an earlier diagnosis of the disease or allowed her to beat it once it was diagnosed. I don't think I have ever cried more than when I got the message that she had died. She was only seventeen.

Today, news commentators tell us that the war in Syria is winding down. They say that the revolution is over. I reject that view. As long as there is injustice, people will resist. As long as people are denied freedom and dignity, they will rise up to demand it. If they are beaten down, they will rise up again.

But there is still a long way to go before my people can live with freedom and dignity.

Today, nearly seven million Syrians are refugees outside the country. About another seven million are internally displaced inside Syria. Inside and outside the country, the number of Syrian children not in school is estimated at nearly 2.5 million. People say that these kids risk becoming a "lost generation." I say that we are not lost. We are the greatest hope for the future of a strong and free Syria. We only need the world to invest in that hope by helping us get access to education.

With education, there is nothing that refugee kids can't achieve. I thought about this a few months ago, when Zayn, my UNICEF colleague in Jordan, sent me a message. She explained that Zaatari had recently hosted some high-level foreign delegation, just like the ones I used to meet. They visited the same school that I had attended in the camp. The visitors asked the students what they wanted to be when they grew up, exactly as I remember such delegations asking us.

"A doctor," one girl said.

"A teacher," said another.

And then a third girl spoke up: "I want to be like Muzoon."

I texted back a smiley face and the message "I want her to be better than Muzoon."

I want her to use *her* voice.

And I want you to use yours.

The kind of world we want needs all of us.

MUZOON ALMELLEHAN is an internationally recognized activist for education, refugees, and the rights of girls and women. She works with UNICEF as a Goodwill Ambassador, the first with official refugee status. She was named one of *Glamour* magazine's Women of the Year and one of *Teen Vogue*'s 21 Under 21.

Muzoon now lives in Newcastle, England, with her family and recently graduated from Newcastle University.

You can read more about Muzoon's work with UNICEF at unicef.org/goodwill-ambassadors/muzoon-almellehan and watch her Tedx talk at ted.com/talks/muzoon_almellehan_why _i_carried_my_school_books_out_of_syria.

WENDY PEARLMAN is a professor of political science at Northwestern University and the author of four books. Wendy's book *We Crossed a Bridge and It Trembled: Voices from Syria* is a collection of firsthand testimonials that chronicle the Syrian revolution, war, and refugee crisis through the stories of people who lived them.

You can read more about Wendy and her body of work at sites.northwestern.edu/wendypearlman/bio/.